The No-Nonsense Guide to

WOMEN'S RIGHTS

'Publishers have created lists of short books that discuss the questions that your average [electoral] candidate will only ever touch if armed with a slogan and a soundbite. Together [such books] hint at a resurgence of the grand educational tradition... Closest to the hot headline issues are *The No-Nonsense Guides*. These target those topics that a large army of voters care about, but that politicos evade. Arguments, figures and documents combine to prove that good journalism is far too important to be left to (most) journalists.'

Boyd Tonkin,
The Independent,
London

About the author
Nikki van der Gaag is a freelance writer, editor and evaluator on development issues. Prior to this she was editorial director at the Panos Institute and co-editor with the *New Internationalist*. She specializes in gender, poverty, human rights and refugees.

Other titles in the series
The No-Nonsense Guide to Animal Rights
The No-Nonsense Guide to Climate Change
The No-Nonsense Guide to Conflict and Peace
The No-Nonsense Guide to Fair Trade
The No-Nonsense Guide to Globalization
The No-Nonsense Guide to Global Terrorism
The No-Nonsense Guide to Human Rights
The No-Nonsense Guide to International Development
The No-Nonsense Guide to International Migration
The No-Nonsense Guide to Islam
The No-Nonsense Guide to Science
The No-Nonsense Guide to Sexual Diversity
The No-Nonsense Guide to Tourism
The No-Nonsense Guide to the United Nations
The No-Nonsense Guide to World Health
The No-Nonsense Guide to World History
The No-Nonsense Guide to World Poverty

About the New Internationalist
The **New Internationalist** is an independent not-for-profit publishing co-operative. Our mission is to report on issues of global justice. We publish informative current affairs and popular reference titles, complemented by world food, photography and gift books as well as calendars, diaries, maps and posters – all with a global justice world view.

If you like this *No-Nonsense Guide* you'll also enjoy the **New Internationalist** magazine. Each month it takes a different subject such as *Trade Justice*, *Nuclear Power* or *Iran*, exploring and explaining the issues in a concise way; the magazine is full of photos, charts and graphs as well as music, film and book reviews, country profiles, interviews and news.

To find out more about the **New Internationalist**, visit our website at
www.newint.org

The  to

WOMEN'S
RIGHTS

Nikki van der Gaag

ST. AGNES ACADEMY-
ST. DOMINIC SCHOOL
LIBRARY

5 2189 0041 1 4656
323.34
G11n   2-5-09

The No-Nonsense Guide to Women's Rights
First published in the UK by
New Internationalist™ Publications Ltd
Oxford OX4 1BW, UK
trothw@newint.org
www.newint.org
New Internationalist is a registered trade mark.

First printed 2004. New edition 2008.

Cover image: Gabe Palmer/Corbis.

© Nikki van der Gaag

The right of Nikki van der Gaag to be identified as the author of this work has
been asserted in accordance with Copyright, Designs and Patents Act 1998.

All rights reserved. No part of this book may be reproduced, stored in a
retrieval system or transmitted, in any form or by any means, electronic,
electrostatic, magnetic tape, mechanical, photocopying, recording or
otherwise, without prior permission in writing of the Publisher.

Series editor: Troth Wells
Design by New Internationalist Publications Ltd.

Type by Avocet Typeset, Chilton, Aylesbury, Bucks.

 Printed on recycled paper by T J Press International, Cornwall, UK who
hold environmental accreditation ISO 14001.

British Library Cataloguing-in-Publication Data.
A catalogue record for this book is available from the British Library.

Library of Congress Cataloguing-in-Publication Data.
A catalogue for this book is available from the Library of Congress.

ISBN - 978 1 904456 99 5

Foreword

DURING THE LAST decades feminist movements in the West and the East, in the North and the South, have witnessed a serious backlash. This applies also to the feminist movement in the United States. Young girls and women under the influence of the educational system and media have abandoned the struggle which their mothers and grandmothers began in the defence of women's rights. Books have been written by American women who extol the virtues of motherhood and enjoin women to revert to the natural functions, namely rearing their children and caring for their husbands and family.

Some of these books have been translated into Arabic in recent years and have met with enthusiastic support from the authorities and from intellectuals, both men and women, who move in their circles. They have showered praise on these 'new' American women writers who have returned to the family, to the movements of so-called women's liberation, which spread to many countries during the middle of the 20th century. Language is often used against women and the poor in every country, especially in our countries, the so-called 'Global South'. Today the word 'liberation' means military and economic occupation in Iraq and Afghanistan. The word 'peace' means war, and 'terror' includes the massacre of Palestinian women and children under Israeli occupation. 'Development' means neo-colonialism, robbing people's economic and intellectual riches in Africa, Asia and Latin America.

We need to unveil the words used by global and local governments, by their media and education. Women and the poor, in almost all countries, in the South and North – but especially in the South – are subjected to a capitalist masculine system based on power and double standards in all domains of life, economic, political, sexual, religious and psychological; at the global, national, family and personal level.

Poor women and children suffer most in this unjust world. They are the first to be dismissed from paid work in any economic crisis. They are the first to die of hunger or poverty. Of the two billion people suffering poverty, 70 per cent are women. Two-thirds of illiterate adults are women. The gender gap is increasing in all areas and there's a growing backlash against women's rights in the South and the North. Women's employment rates have been declining steadily in most countries. Women are obliged to be isolated or veiled for religious reasons or to expose their bodies for commercial profit. Women's make-up, earrings, high heels, submissive smiles are back. Feminine is good, feminism is evil.

'Family Values' are back in fashion. New laws or family codes have emerged in some countries to give men more power over women and to emphasize traditional gender roles.

The capitalist masculine system benefits a small upper-class group of business and top governmental men and women. Power and money work together to exploit the majority of people, especially poor women and their children.

Nikki van der Gaag's book is refreshing and enjoyable. In it she has made a special effort to correct many of the misconceptions and biases related to the feminist movement, to link the liberation of women who constitute half of society to the liberation of men, and to the dispossessed majority living on the earth.

Nawal El Saadawi
Author of *Woman at Point Zero*
Cairo

CONTENTS

Introduction

MY SON GEORGE, aged 17, can't understand what all the fuss is about. 'Why are you so obsessed with women's rights?' he asks me. From his point of view, his mum and dad are both working, his sister Rosa is doing well at university, his friends who are girls do just as well or better than the boys at school. And he has done the suffragettes at least three times in class. Women's rights just aren't an issue.

I could tell him stories about girls younger than him from the recent report I have been writing. About Mariatu, for example, who lives in Sierra Leone. During the war she was captured by rebels. She says: 'Life was terrible there. There was no food, we were constantly moving from one place to another. I tried to escape but one of the rebels caught me and raped me. I escaped from them again with a group of other girls. We walked all the way from Freetown to Bombali – about 150 miles. When I arrived back in Bombali I managed to find my parents and returned to live with them. But my stomach started protruding and it was then that I realised that I was pregnant. I was 13 years old.'

Or closer to home, I could tell him about the women I have been working with here in Britain; women living on the breadline, many of them single parents because they had the courage to leave a violent relationship. They struggle to find enough to pay for Christmas presents and school trips for their kids. They are smart and ingenious and amazing at making a little money go a long way. One of their main problems is that they don't feel that their skills and experience are valued; that they do not have people's respect.

Or I could quote him some statistics; that even in Britain women working full-time still earn 17 per cent less than men and the numbers of women in top executive positions are actually going down; that globally women remain woefully under-represented in parliament – 23 countries have fewer than five per cent of women in parliament, eight have none at all. How millions of girls are married off and having babies before their bodies are fully-grown; that women make up two-thirds of those who can't read and write and one in three women suffers from abuse and violence. But perhaps the best argument is that standing up for women's rights also benefits boys and men.

We are certainly going to have some interesting discussions. And all in all, I am happy to be the mother who is obsessed with women's rights.

Nikki van der Gaag
Oxford

1 Living in interesting times

'As long as discrimination and inequities remain so commonplace around the world – as long as girls and women are valued less, fed less, fed last, overworked, underpaid, not schooled and subjected to violence in and out of their homes – the potential of the human family to create a peaceful, prosperous world will not be realized.' HILLARY CLINTON, US PRESIDENTIAL CANDIDATE.[1]

THERE IS AN old Chinese saying: 'May you live in interesting times.' Women today are living in interesting times and it is not yet clear whether this is a curse or a blessing. Thanks to the women's movement, gender equality, at least in theory, is firmly on the agenda and has made a real difference to many women's lives – more girls are being educated, women are living longer, there are more female parliamentarians than ever before; more women are working, and, importantly, women themselves are more aware of their rights.

On the other hand, for millions of women around the world, life continues to become even harder. There are still 1.3 billion people living in poverty and the majority of these are women. So are two-thirds of illiterate adults. Women and children are the main victims of conflict and are increasingly targeted for rape and sexual assault. One in three women worldwide will experience violence in her lifetime. Even in the rich world, the pay gap between men and women persists. In addition, girls and women increasingly have to struggle with cultural constraints that place them firmly back in traditional roles in the kitchen. And this is not just in countries where extreme versions of religion dictate what they may and may not do. Even in the US, the undertow is there, as Hillary Clinton found in her 2008 campaign.

Changes for the better

- More women are working – since 1980, the growth in women's labor force has been substantially higher than that of men in every region of the world except Africa.
- More girls are being educated – by 2005, 63 per cent of countries had equal numbers of boys and girls in primary school and 37 per cent at secondary.
- Women are living longer – today, in 30 countries, female life expectancy at birth now exceeds 80 years.*
- Women are having fewer children – 50 per cent of women now have access to modern contraception.
- There are more women in politics than ever before and more women at grassroots level as well. There are six female presidents.
- Legislation, from international to local, is recognizing that women's rights need to be protected.
- There are more liberal marriage laws in some countries and in the rich world/North the average age of marriage is going up.
- Lesbian women in some countries have more rights than they did before – homosexuality is legal in 111 countries and a number of Northern countries now have some legislation recognizing same-sex relationships.
- Female genital cutting has been outlawed in six African countries.
- Women are more aware of their rights, even in poor communities.

*www.un.org/esa/population/publications/worldageing19502050/pdf/8chapteri.pdf

Backlash

Much of this seems to be part of a continuing backlash, fueled at least in part by George W Bush's term in office and the American right wing – see for example in the next chapter on the continuing impact of the 'global gag' rule which prevents US money going to any organizations which are said to be linked to abortion. It is estimated that this will mean two million more unwanted pregnancies, 800,000 more abortions, 4,700 more dead mothers and 77,000 deaths of children under five.

In work, in many countries in the North, the gender gap in earnings persists – in the US in 2003, on average, women earned 75.5 per cent of men's wages. This was down for the first time in four years.[2]

Hillary-haters

As Hillary Clinton contemplated being America's first woman president, she also had to put up with a barrage of insults – simply because she is female. For example, in November 2007, a woman asked Arizona Senator and Republican contender for President John McCain: 'How do we beat the bitch?' Momentarily nonplussed, McCain came back with: 'That's a good question', and proceeded to explain how he would beat [Ms Clinton]. The following week saw the clip being viewed almost a million times on YouTube.

Anti-Hillary websites proliferate on Facebook. They focus on her role in the kitchen and not the political arena, and some are violent. One is 'Hillary Clinton: Stop Running for President and Make Me a Sandwich', with more than 23,000 members and 2,200 'wall posts'. Another, with about 13,000 members, is 'Life's a bitch, why vote for one? Anti-Hillary '08'.

But it is not just aberrant voters and social networking sites that buy into the anti-woman propaganda. On his radio show, which reaches 14.5 million people, Rush Limbaugh talks about Clinton's 'testicle lock box'. On his MSNBC show, Tucker Carlson says, 'There's just something about her that feels castrating, overbearing and scary.' In her review of a recent book called *Thirty Ways of Looking at Hillary: Reflections by women writers*, Susan Faludi writes: 'Let's imagine this book's concept – 30 well-known women writers talk about how they "feel" about Hillary Clinton – applied to 30 male writers and a male presidential candidate. Adjusting for gender, the essay titles would now read: 'Barack's Underpants', 'Elect Brother Frigidaire', 'Mephistopheles for President', 'The Road to Codpiece-Gate', and so on. Inside, we would find ruminations on the male candidate's doggy looks and flabby pectorals... We would hear a great deal about how [Barack Obama] made them feel about themselves as men and whether they could see their manhood reflected in the politician's testosterone displays. And we would hear virtually nothing about their stand on political issues.'

If Hillary were a man it would be a very different story.

www.observer.com
http://seattletimes.nwsource.com

In Britain, women working full-time earn on average 17 per cent less an hour than men working full-time. Their part-time sisters average 36 per cent less an hour than men working full-time. The Fawcett Society, which campaigns for women's equality, estimates that at current rates of change it will take more than 140 years to close all women's pay gaps.

Politically, worldwide, we now have six women presidents, which is great, but this is still only six out of 194, which is a pretty poor percentage. In 2007, only 19 countries had achieved the benchmark of 30 per cent representation of women in parliament and this number actually fell from 20 in 2006. As the chapter on poverty, development and work (chapter 3) shows, aid money targeted at women is actually falling, despite all the world's grand promises on gender equality.

In the Muslim world, fundamentalists' narrow interpretations of the Qur'an amount to an attack on women's rights. 'In any situation where religious fundamentalism is on the rise it will always impact on women because at the heart of the religious fundamentalist agenda is the control of women, of reproductive rights and of the family,' says Pragna Patel of Southall Black Sisters in the UK.[3]

In some cases, beliefs and practices are being dredged up from the past by fundamentalists and recast, sometimes in countries where they were never common practice. In Sri Lanka, for example, some groups demanded the introduction of female genital cutting (FGC) as an 'Islamic duty', despite the fact that no-one in Sri Lanka had ever practiced FGC and that it has nothing to do with Islam.

The new administrations in Iraq and Afghanistan have seen few women in positions of power. In Afghanistan, despite the emphasis on women, they have been largely excluded from the rebuilding of their country. Iraq, once renowned for its relative freedom for women, is seeing women attacked and murdered in the street.

In the West, some men – and women – feel strongly that women's rights are only being granted at the expense of men's rights. The UK Men's Movement is at the strident end of this: 'We regard the assertion that women are disadvantaged as The Big Lie of our time. And feminism is based on The Big Lie. There

Requiem for a brave woman

Sahar Hussein al-Haideri, 45, an Iraqi reporter working in the Mosul region, was murdered outside her home on 7 June 2007.

Sahar al-Haideri had to die because she was a journalist – an Iraqi journalist who dared to ask questions, and who gave a voice to Iraqis who do not want their country to be torn apart by sectarian violence or ruled by terror imposed by al-Qaeda's franchise organizations.

Haideri, 45, reported from her home city of Mosul, a troubled place considered Iraq's second most dangerous location for journalists after Baghdad... She described how female lecturers and civil servants were being targeted and killed.

'The intimidation and attacks have forced other women in Mosul to give up going to work,' she wrote.

Staying home was not an option she considered for herself. She went where no foreign journalist could go any more – into the streets, shops and restaurants of her volatile city.

Haideri was a tough reporter but also a caring wife and mother of four. The human touch was never missing from her work. Her stories always reflected this concern for people's lives – shopkeepers and teachers; mothers, fathers and children; students, hairdressers and janitors.

George Packer, a reporter for *The New Yorker*, recently wrote in the *Dangerous Assignments* magazine, 'The campaign of killing – conducted largely by insurgents and militias – has been systematic. Its purpose is to make journalism impossible.'

Haideri was aware of the risk her work entailed. Every journalist in Iraq knows he or she might be killed at any moment, and repeated threats are commonplace. Many have fled the country, while some leave temporarily in the hope of coming back as soon as the situation improves.

As we mourn her death, the best tribute we can pay her is to remember that she is not the only one on the hit-list. There are many more journalists in Iraq who need our help if we want them to stand up against those trying to silence them.

'May God save female journalists, most of whom work anonymously for fear of being killed for no other crime than telling the truth,' Haideri said in remarks that went out on the Institute for War and Peace (IWPR)'s radio show *The Other Half*. Iraqi journalists need more support of a worldly nature, too.

From an article by Susanne Fischer, IWPR's Iraq country director, in IWPR'S Iraqi Crisis Report No 233 Part 2, 12 June 2007.
http://iwpr.net/?p=icr&s=f&o=336147&apc_state=henh

can be no greater folly or degeneracy than to provide further support, via Ministers for Women etc, to the most privileged group in our society – women – while denying the disadvantaged, suppressed and persecuted group – men – any representation at all. Feminism is about women getting something for nothing. The question of whether "feminism has gone too far" is perhaps less important than "why feminism was established at all". Feminism is an aberration, like Nazism and communism – a blight on our society.'

They are not the only ones to see feminism, and the gains women have made, in this light. Some of this may have been fueled by the focus on gender – one research study in four countries in Africa shows widespread confusion about the term 'gender'. The report notes: 'Gender legislation and shifts in gender relations have had some positive effects, giving women in these countries access to new resources and activities, seeing them participate more fully in public life, supporting them as household heads and so on. It has also had many negative effects, including increasing men's hostility towards change, and exacerbating tensions between women and men in families.'[4]

Sometimes this resentment spills into outright violence. A South African report suggests that high levels of violence against women recently reported in some studies may be partly fueled by male backlash against the progress women have made.[5] Researchers have referred to this as 'neo-patriarchy' – a new attempt to exert male authority, in this case through a culture of sexual violence.[6]

Finding a new word for feminism

One of the problems is that women's rights are seen by some – or used by some – as a largely Western agenda. Karma Nabulsi, a politics research fellow at Oxford University in Britain, says: 'When the political élites face battles with the Islamists, all of their opponents' arguments are being cast as "We want to get rid of the West", and women's rights are part of that.'

This restriction of women's rights as part of an

anti-West agenda is not found only in the Muslim world. In Uganda, which has a positive record on women's rights, an amendment to the Land Act which would give married women the rights to own land was rejected by President Museveni on the grounds that he wanted to save the world from the mistakes of the West. 'It is like telling the Karimojong [nomadic herders] that Parliament had passed a Bill allowing women to share cows,' he said. 'There will be a civil war'.[7] The Women of Uganda network says: 'His ideological stance is trapped in a 1960s' time-warp, and the questions he raises on gender are out of step with what is now the general understanding of what constitutes gender issues. The President's analysis of issues is contradictory in that while he is loathsome of Western values, he projects a social evolution that is determinedly Western and capitalist.'[8]

Suddenly, women's rights have become an import, along with Coca-Cola, Levi jeans and pornography. The irony is that a huge amount of the thinking and the pushing through of women's issues over the last 10 or 20 years has come from women in the countries of the Majority World/South, who saw the inequalities with which they lived and decided to do something about it. 'The notion that feminism is Western is still bandied about by those ignorant of history or who perhaps more willfully employ it in a delegitimizing way,' says scholar Margot Badran. 'Feminism, however, is a plant that only grows in its own soil.'[9]

For some Muslim women, veiling has become part of a wider statement against the West. Where 25 years ago, liberation meant throwing off the *hijab* [veil], today, women who would never have worn the veil before are doing so, in large numbers.

The aftermath of 11 September 2001 continues to haunt us, pushing a security agenda that undermines civil liberties and forcing people to choose specific identities that separate them into narrow groupings

– 'with us' or 'against us', Muslim or Christian, black or white.

In many Muslim countries, women are arguing for the right to define what it means to be Muslim in their own terms. Saad Hamid, a lawyer advising the Palestinian women's legal reform movement in Gaza, says that many in the Arab world are searching for avenues to advance women's rights within the context of Islam. 'Solutions to 90 per cent of the problems exist within Islam if you want to find them,' says Hamid. 'What we're trying to do is show that there are different schools of Islamic jurisprudence. Saying I know nothing about it, and I want to banish it and have purely secular laws, that's ridiculous.'[10]

Writer Leila Ahmed noted in her novel *A Border Passage*: 'Generations of astute, thoughtful women, listening to the Qur'an, understood perfectly well its essential themes and its faith. And looking around them, they understood perfectly well, too, what a travesty men had made of it.' 'My problem is not with Islam, it is with the culture of patriarchy,' says Iranian human-rights lawyer Shirin Ebadi.

One of the early feminists, Rebecca West, may have been British, but she summed up quite accurately the essence of feminism and what it still means for most women wherever they live in the world when she said in 1913: 'I myself have never been able to find out precisely what feminism is; I only know that people call me a feminist whenever I express sentiments that differentiate me from a doormat.'

It is interesting that in the last few years, young women in particular have been starting to call them selves feminists. Women's organizations in Britain and the US have produced T-shirts proclaiming; 'I am a feminist' and a Google search reveals a number of

Turning into a Muslim

I was at a conference in Birmingham which I went into as normal, my usual mixed-up self, full of odd thoughts and random worries. As that day, 11 September, unfolded, I turned into a Muslim. Of course I was born a Muslim in Iran, I grew up as one under the Shah in the 1950s and 1960s, but I had never really thought about it, it wasn't an issue, just there in the background. But after that conference I took a taxi back to the station. The driver was a Muslim, and when he realized I was one as well, he slowed right down. He asked me what we could do, as Muslims, about this terrible event, and about our own position. We progressed across that city at around ten miles an hour – and talked and talked.

I am a scholar, a teacher, somebody who engages in arguments, in dialogue, reasoned debate. For the first time, I was someone who had started getting hate mail. It came from people who had just seen that I was on TV or on the radio, without knowing what I had said beyond maybe a sound bite. Thus I was categorized as Muslim, troublesome, by people who I had never met and who had never heard what I have to say in any depth. I would get these vile postcards, and I remember my head of department scribbling on one of them: 'We don't all think like this my dear!'

Now there have been notions and proposals about solidarity kicking around in the Muslim community for years. People talked about it, but, in extremis, it began to make a sort of sense. I had not made a habit of announcing my identity, it was not relevant, but as that period unfolded, I felt I no longer had any choice. For years I had been denouncing the policies and practice of places like Saudi Arabia, but suddenly there were all sorts of issues on which I felt it inappropriate to voice criticisms. Those times didn't seem the right time.

It has also meant I found myself in meetings alongside all sorts of strange bedfellows, people who I had, in some cases, previously refused to be in the same room with. I chaired meetings where I found myself in some degree of sympathy with fundamentalists there. Why was that? Because we had been categorized as Muslim terrorists together by the outside world.

Maybe it is because I am used to working within liberal academia, where it is less of an issue, than in other harsher places where Muslims are trying to make themselves invisible, but all of this has brought out the Muslim in me, an attitude of 'I will face you all'. I object to being cowed.

Haleh Afshar is professor of Middle Eastern politics at the University of York.

The Guardian 11 September 2002.

new books with a feminist title or agenda – *Full Frontal Feminism: A Young Woman's Guide to why Feminism Matters* by Jessica Valenti,[11] is one. Valenti notes that 'Feminism is a pretty amazing thing,' and says: 'I don't know why I didn't call myself a feminist until I was in college. I certainly was one way before then. I think we all are.

'I mean, really, what young girl *hasn't* thought at some point that some sexist bullshit is completely unfair to women? The problem seems to be putting a name on that feeling. "Feminism" is just too scary and loaded a word for some women. Which is really too bad. Because feminism is a pretty amazing thing.

'When you're a feminist, day-to-day life is better. You make better decisions. You have better sex. You understand the struggles you're up against and how best to handle them. I wrote *Full Frontal Feminism* because I spent a really long time feeling completely confused about why more young women wouldn't embrace something that to me was clearly the greatest thing ever...

'Most important perhaps, was my desire to write something that explained not only why feminism is so necessary and relevant, but also why it's so damn cool.'

On the other hand, some young women think that

Defining feminism

The word '*feminisme*' was first coined in France in the 1880s, and referred to a social movement for women's rights. It was not used widely by women until the 1970s when the Women's Liberation movement used it to mean anyone who challenged gender relations; 'the principle that women should have economic and social rights equal to those of men'. Feminism then became multiple 'feminisms' as Third World women, women of color, lesbian women, and working-class women claimed it as their own and moved it beyond a social and political movement to one claiming economic justice as well. By the mid 1990s the media in the North heralded a 'post-feminist' era. But many of the basic feminist demands have still not been met.

Women's rights 900 BC-2008
900 BC

In ancient Sumer (Iraq), Egypt and Japan, adult women can own property, play active roles in the marketplace and even be clerics. In the Andes, giving birth is seen as equivalent to taking a prisoner of war and death in childbirth is as honorable as death in battle. In pre-colonial Latin America, some native cultures practice what anthropologists call 'gender parallelism' valuing equally the distinct and overlapping tasks performed by men and women. The agrarian societies that followed tend to be less egalitarian.

In the **1400s**, trade brings new status to women in some countries. In Nigeria, among the Igbo, a wealthy woman can buy a 'wife' to work with her and Yoruba women elect their own female representatives to protect their trading interests.

1776 During the French Revolution, working women march on Versailles to demand bread. In 1791 this inspires French playwright Olympe de Gouges to issue the 'Declaration of the Rights of Woman and the Female Citizen'. She is executed by guillotine when the French Revolution rejects demands for women's rights.

1759-1797 In Britain, Mary Wollstonecraft rejects conventional family authority, believes in female education, and bears a child out of wedlock. In 1792 she writes *A Vindication of the Rights of Woman* which becomes a catalyst for much later feminist thinking.

1848 The world's first women's rights convention (with men as well as women) is held in Seneca Falls, New York, setting the agenda for the women's rights movement.

1850s In Brazil, women's urban newspapers such as *O Jornal das Senhoras* (Ladies' Journal) complain that marriage is 'an unbearable tyranny' and women deserve 'a just enjoyment of their rights'.

1880-1890 The Japanese women's movement is founded. Kishida Toshiko is jailed for a week after calling for women's horizons to be 'as large and free as the world itself'. The Government bans women's political participation during the 1890s.

1861 In Russia, the emancipation of serfs raises women's expectations of equality.

1893 New Zealand becomes the first country to give women the vote.

1896 In the US, the National Association of Colored Women unites Black women's organizations, with Mary Church Terrell its first president. The NACW becomes a major vehicle for reform during the next 40 years.

1890-1923 In the late 1800s Islam is used to justify the education of women. In 1923 Huda Sha'rawawi founds the Egyptian Feminist Union. Women are at the forefront of the battle for independence from the British.

1911 Socialists observe 8 March as a day to honor the women who had organized strikes for better working conditions in the 19th and 20th centuries. In Mexico Jovita and Soledad Pena organize *La Liga Femenil Mexicanista* (League of Mexican Feminists).

1913 In South Africa traditional women's organizations such as Manyano act as savings clubs for poor women. They are also at the forefront of the fight against apartheid.

1920 In the US, African American women meet to discuss how they can 'stand side by side with women of the white race and work for the full emancipation of all women' (Lugenia Burns Hope).

1926 In Turkey, as part of his program for modernization, Kemal Atatürk abolishes polygamy, makes schools and universities coeducational, gives women political rights and recognizes the equal rights of women in divorce, custody, and inheritance.

1929 The 'women's war' in Nigeria is a response among Igbo women's trading networks to the planned imposition by the British rulers of a new tax on women's property. The British put down the revolt by firing into the crowd, killing 50 women and injuring 50.

1941 In the US, almost seven million women take jobs during the war; two million as industrial 'Rosie the Riveters' and 400,000 joining the military.

1947 Gandhi expresses strong opposition to male domination of women, and India's first Prime Minister, Jawaharlal Nehru, calls for equal educational and work opportunities for women and men. Nationalists adopt the slogan 'India cannot be free until its women are free and women cannot be free until India is free.' The 1947 constitution guarantees equality between the sexes.

1948 In Egypt, Doria Shafik forms the Daughters of the Nile Union. In 1951 she organizes an invasion of the Egyptian parliament by women and in 1953 creates a women's political party that is then suppressed by the government.

1959 In eastern Nigeria 2,000 women protest their declining status by occupying and setting fire to a market. They negotiate a resolution that eliminates all foreign courts and schools and expels all foreigners.

1977 Argentinean women constitute themselves into the 'Mothers of the Plaza de Mayo' to defy the murderous military junta that seized power from President Isabel Peron.

1975-2001 The birth and growth of the feminist movement. First international women's conference in Mexico, launching the United Nations Decade for Women and the formation of women's groups all over the world, including feminist newspapers, student organizations, professional women and lesbian feminists. Followed by conferences in Copenhagen (1980), Nairobi (1985) and Beijing (1995). Women's rights become enshrined in law in many countries.

2001-2008 Women continue to organize for their rights, while at the same time facing a backlash against their successes.

lap-dancing and wearing as few clothes as possible is sexual liberation. Erica Jong, feminist and campaigner, on the 30th anniversary of her novel *Fear of Flying*, said: 'The women who buy the idea that flaunting your breasts with sequins is power – I mean, I'm for all that stuff – but let's not get so into the tits and ass that we don't notice how far we haven't come. Let's not confuse that with real power. I don't like to see women fooled.'[12]

It may be that it is time to open our eyes, reclaim women's rights, and perhaps to reinvent the word feminism as something universal; to take it back to its roots and to make it something that women can claim as their own. Only then will things really begin to change.

1 Speech in Beijing at the United Nations Fourth World Conference on Women, 1995, www.famousquotes.me.uk/speeches/Hillary-Clinton **2** www.usatoday.com/money/workplace/2004-08-26-women_x.htm. **3** *Trouble and Strife* 43, Summer 2002. **4** *Living Gender in African Organizations and Communities: Stories from The Gambia, Rwanda, Uganda and Zambia*, Senorina Wendoh and Tina Wallace. May 2006, www.transformafrica.org/docs/gender_research_report.pdf. **5** Anderson N et al, 2000, 'Beyond Victims and Villains: The Culture of Sexual Violence in South Johannesburg', Community Information and Transparency Foundation (CIET) Africa. **6** *Beyond victims and villains: addressing sexual violence in the education sector*, Panos, 2003. **7** *The East African*, 13 March 2000. **8** www.wougnet.org/Alerts/drbresponseEK.html. **9** http://weekly.ahram.org.eg/2002/569/cu1.htm. **10** Karma Nabulsi and Saad Hamid are quoted in www.christiansciencemonitor.org. **11** *Full Frontal Feminism: A Young Woman's Guide to why Feminism Matters*, Jessica Valenti, Seal Press, 2007. **12** Quoted in *Female Chauvinist Pigs: women and the rise of raunch culture*, Ariel Levy, Pocket Books, 2005.

2 Birth and death

'Too many women still die during childbirth or soon after and actually we know the solutions, we know what to do. It is just a matter of getting it done... we must have this sense of urgency, we must really work together and we must take action on the ground.'
DR MARGARET CHAN, WHO DIRECTOR-GENERAL.[1]

From birth to death, women still face unnecessary dangers to their health, just because they are women. Female fetuses are aborted because they are female, hundreds of thousands of women die in childbirth, and increasing numbers live in the shadow of the HIV/AIDS epidemic.

NO WOMAN TODAY should die unnecessarily in childbirth or of pregnancy-related causes. And yet 1,500 women die like this every single day; in 2005 this amounted to more than half a million deaths. Eleven countries accounted for almost 65 per cent of global maternal deaths, also known as maternal mortality. India had the largest number (117,000), followed by Nigeria (59,000), the Democratic Republic of the Congo (32,000) and Afghanistan (26,000). Ninety-nine per cent of deaths occur in developing countries; maternal deaths are also one of the most obvious indicators of the widening gap between rich and poor. Poor women and those from minority groups in the North are also more at risk than their richer sisters – in the US, five white women die for every 100,000 births, but the figures rise to 10 if you are a Hispanic woman, 12 if you are Native American and 20 if you are African-American.[2] And for every woman who dies, many millions more suffer illness and ill-health, often long-term, as a result of giving birth.

The UN's Millennium Development Goals set a target for an annual decline of 5.5 per cent per year

Birth and death

State of the World's Children 2008, UNICEF.

Table 1 – Mothers' demise

Women in sub-Saharan Africa are more likely to die from pregnancy/childbirth-related illnesses than elsewhere in the world.

Annual number of deaths of women from pregnancy-related causes per 100,000 births, 2005

Sub-Saharan Africa	920
South Asia	500
Middle East and North Africa	210
East Asia and Pacific	150
Latin America and Caribbean	130
CEE/CIS*	46
Industrialized Countries	8

*Central and Eastern Europe/Commonwealth of Independent States.

in maternal mortality ratios between 1990 and 2015, but recent figures show that while there is a decline, it is currently less than one per cent. The World Health Organization (WHO) notes that: 'Countries with the highest initial levels of mortality have made virtually no progress over the past 15 years.'[3]

So why are so many women still dying in the process of becoming mothers? Poverty is one simple answer. If you are poor, you are more likely to die giving birth than if you are rich. Poor women, and women in poor countries, often have neither the resources nor the knowledge to prevent such deaths. Often they also have little access to clinics or hospitals, including maternity services and antenatal care.

Resources are another. Almost half the maternal health services in a study of 49 developing countries were judged so poorly resourced that they could not carry out one or more of the lifesaving procedures they were meant to offer. To prevent these deaths, women need access to family planning, and high-quality pregnancy and delivery care, including emergency obstetric care. Women also need to be able to get to these services and use them. Research has shown that female education and gender equality can help empower women to have the knowledge and make the

A tale of two pregnancies

Journalist Joanna Moorhead visited two mothers-to-be in two different worlds. This is an extract from her report.

Niger

Salawa Abdou is 20 and expecting her second child in a few weeks' time – she is not sure exactly when. Salawa has had no antenatal care. She dreads the delivery because she endured a very difficult, 48-hour labor with her son, Banani, two years ago. 'It was very painful and very long,' she says. 'I was at home and we tried everything, but the baby wouldn't come out. It was terrible. In the end I was lucky, but I worry a lot about what is going to happen this time.' Death is a real possibility for women who get into difficulties giving birth in Fardun Sofo: Zeinabou Abdou, the village's traditional birth attendant, has years of experience but no drugs and no equipment except for a packet of razor blades for cutting the umbilical cord. If Salawa needs medical help, she will be put on a cart and pulled by horse to the small maternity unit in Matamy, 9 miles/15km away. So far this year, two mothers-to-be, out of a population of around 400, have died making the journey.

Sweden

Lisa Klercker is 35, and 30 weeks pregnant with her third child. She lives in a Stockholm suburb. Her other children are Ebba, seven, and Max, four. She has monthly pre-natal check-ups at the mothercare centre near her home, and she will give birth in hospital. Lisa says that she is quietly confident that the delivery will go well. 'We do have friends whose babies have had problems, so I don't take anything for granted,' she says. If there are difficulties, she knows she will get the best possible care: before Ebba's delivery, the baby's heartbeat dipped suddenly, and she was transferred to hospital by helicopter. 'It was quite dramatic but the medical staff were really calm. They made me feel everything would turn out OK and it did,' she says. 'What I like about being in hospital is that I know everything I need will be there. I feel I'll be in a safe place, with the best possible care available.' Lisa expects to go home within hours of the delivery, and will then have visits from a team of postnatal midwives to help with any early problems.

Joanna Moorhead, *The Guardian*, 2 October 2006, www.guardian.co.uk

decisions that can save their lives.

All this comes down to priorities. The World Bank has estimated that the financial cost of basic maternal health services in developing countries is $2 per person per year.

The tragedy is that almost all maternal deaths are

ST. AGNES ACADEMY-
ST. DOMINIC SCHOOL
LIBRARY

preventable. The main medical cause of maternal death is severe bleeding. The others are infection, unsafe abortion and eclampsia (convulsions, or seizures, occurring during or immediately after pregnancy). Anemia also poses a risk to pregnant women – in Asia, 60 per cent are anemic, in Africa 52 per cent, in Latin America 39 per cent and in Europe and the US 17 per cent. Basic health facilities and medicines would save nearly all of these lives. But, it seems, women's health is not high on the global agenda – or on national agendas.

Teenage mothers

The younger you are, the more risky pregnancy is – girls aged 10 to 14 are five times more likely to die in pregnancy or childbirth than women in their early twenties. Girls such as 19-year-old Ganga from Nepal continue to suffer because they gave birth so young: 'I married at age 12, before I even had my first period. I am from a lower caste family and I never attended school. We cannot afford nutritious food or a decent house to live in. I have three children – two daughters and a son. My last childbirth was especially difficult – I cannot describe for you how much I suffered during that time. I still feel weak and I look like an old woman. I have enormous awful days in my life.'[4]

Young mothers also face an added risk from malnutrition, anemia, injury and infection. And yet approximately 15 million adolescent girls give birth each year, more than 10 per cent of all births worldwide. Many young women giving birth too early are afflicted with obstetric fistula, the result of trauma during childbirth. Fistula is a tear in the birth canal, either into the rectum or urethra, which constantly leaks bodily wastes. The sufferer is usually ostracized, abandoned and ashamed. Fistula continues to strike 50,000 to 100,000 adolescent girls and women in developing countries each year.[5]

Young mothers

- Complications from pregnancy and childbirth are the leading cause of death among young women aged 15 to 19 in the developing world.
- An estimated 70,000 teenage girls die from these causes each year.
- Teenage girls who get pregnant are twice as likely to die from pregnancy- and childbirth-related conditions and complications than older women.
- Girls who become mothers between 10 and 14 are more than five times more likely to die than those aged 20-24.
- Babies born to teenage mothers have a 50 per cent higher chance of dying before their first birthday than babies born to women in their 20s.
- More than 750,000 teenagers in the developed world will become mothers in the next year.

The State of the World's Mothers 2004, Save the Children US.

Teenage pregnancy is something that occurs all over the world. There are more teenage mothers in the US than in any other industrialized country. The rate is two and a half times that of the UK, 10 times that of Japan and the Netherlands and 17 times that of the Republic of Korea. Having a baby as a teenager means that you are twice as likely to end up living in poverty as your peers who are not mothers.[6] A very high proportion of teenage pregnancies are unwanted. Each year, teenagers seek about four million abortions.

So why are young girls having babies? In some countries, religious and cultural traditions insist on early marriage. Every year 82 million young women between the ages of 10 and 17 are married. More than 50 countries allow marriage at 16 or younger, and seven allow it as young as 12. In sub-Saharan Africa, more than 50 per cent of women give birth before the age of 20. And in other countries, young people are having sex earlier and earlier, partly because cultures are increasingly sexualized in advertising, films and the media. The messages of safe sex and pregnancy prevention are clearly not getting across to this group. In the US, 22 per cent of 15- to 19-year-olds who have sexual intercourse become pregnant.

Birth and death

Fertility and family planning

'A woman's health prospects are transformed if she can decide whether and when she wants to have children,' says Margaret Catley-Carlson, President of the Population Council.[7]

Overall, women are having fewer children than their mothers and grandmothers. In the last 30 years, women's use of contraceptives has increased dramatically. More than 50 per cent of the world's women now use modern contraceptive methods.[8] Many more would prefer to be able to plan their pregnancies. But access to modern contraception, medical advice and follow-up are not available to all who want them. Husbands may prevent their wives from using contraception for a variety of reasons, including the argument that she may become 'promiscuous' if she is freed from having to worry about having children.

Contraceptive use is uneven, with women in richer countries and urban areas having the best access, while others spend most of their reproductive lives bearing children every year.

Nearly 230 million women – nearly one in six women of reproductive age – still need the choice of effective family planning in order to space or limit the size of their families. More than 50 per cent of women in some countries report that they would have preferred to postpone or avoid their most recent birth.[9] With so much rhetoric today about choice, it is interesting to note that a woman's right to choose how many children she wants to have hardly exists in many parts of the world.

While men remain reluctant to consider sterilization, despite the fact that the operation is a relatively minor one compared to female sterilization, the latter remains the most common form of contraception. Despite the risk of HIV/AIDs, condoms still make up only 9 per cent of contraceptive methods.

At 30 per cent worldwide, female sterilization

Table 2 – Contraception contradictions

Despite the risk of HIV/AIDs, condoms still make up only 9 per cent of contraceptive methods.

Types of contraception for women

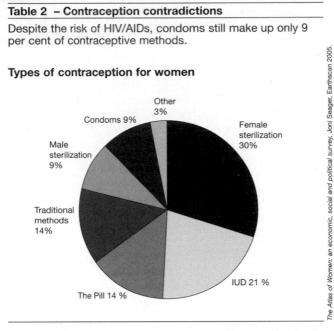

The Atlas of Women: an economic, social and political survey, Joni Seager, Earthscan 2005.

remains the most common contraceptive method – in Australia, 38 per cent of women have been sterilized, in Brazil, 43 per cent and in El Salvador 60 per cent.

Abuses are common; governments of countries like the US, China and India have imposed sterilization on minority or poor women during the last three decades. Male sterilization is a much simpler operation, but is undergone by only a tiny proportion of men, who feel that it somehow challenges their 'manhood'.

Global pharmaceutical companies have marketed unsafe or experimental contraceptives, particularly to poor women. 'Women still face the dilemma that the safest contraceptives are not the most effective, while the most effective are not necessarily the safest,' comments Joni Seager, author of *The Atlas of Women*.

Birth and death

Son preference

'If she has given birth to a son the family will care about her. But if she has given birth to a baby girl they will neglect her. She has to do operation of family planning after giving a birth to a son. But she cannot do operation until she gives a birth to a son. If she gives birth to a girl, she has to continue it till the son is born,' says one woman from Nepal.[10]

The global preference for sons over daughters remains marked. In some places this produces demographic distortion – the biological norm is for 95 girls to be born for every 100 boys, but male infants have a higher mortality rate so by early childhood the numbers should be even. In countries including South Korea, India, China, Bangladesh and Pakistan, there are now as few as 80 girls per 100 boys. About seven per cent of girls under the age of five are 'missing' in China and Korea, and more than four per cent in India and other parts of South Asia.

The availability of genetic testing also means that in some countries it is used to select female fetuses for abortion. In India, genetic testing for sex selection is a booming business. Indian gender-detection clinics drew protests from women's groups, especially after the appearance of advertisements suggesting that it was better to 'spend $38 now to terminate a female fetus than $3,800 later on a daughter's dowry'. A study of amniocentesis procedures conducted in a large Mumbai (Bombay) hospital found that 95.5 per cent of fetuses identified as female were aborted, compared with a far smaller percentage of male fetuses. Without such discrimination,' says the World Bank, 'there would be an estimated 60 to 100 million more women in the world.'[11]

Son preference is not just a Southern phenomenon. Asked how many children he had fathered, the former United States boxing champion Muhammad Ali told an interviewer: 'One boy and seven mistakes.'[12]

Abortion

It has been estimated that almost 40 per cent of pregnancies in the world are unplanned.[13] Of the 45 million unintended pregnancies that are terminated each year, an estimated 19 million take place in unsafe conditions. Approximately 40 per cent of these are performed on young women aged 15 to 24. Unsafe abortion kills an estimated 68,000 women every year globally and accounts for 13 per cent of all pregnancy-related deaths.

One way of reducing levels of abortion is to prevent unwanted pregnancy by making family planning services more accessible. In the Central Asian countries of Kazakhstan, Uzbekistan and Kyrgyzstan, better availability of services and information has increased the use of modern contraception by 30-50 per cent since 1990, and abortion rates have declined by half.[14]

Since the 1980s, pressure from women has led to more liberal abortion laws in some countries. But 25 per cent of the world's women still live in countries where abortion is illegal – or only legal if a woman's life is in danger.

And there has been a backlash in the last 10 years. Rather than a full assault on abortion, the US Right has generally opted for a piecemeal approach, changing a small piece of legislation here and there; enforcing laws which say that women must look at photographs of fetuses before deciding to terminate (Texas' deceptively-named 'Women's Right to Know' act) or enacting laws which mandate punishment for causing harm to a fetus during a crime such as when the mother is beaten (26 states including California). In South Carolina, there was discussion about the erection of a giant model fetus on state grounds. And in Oklahoma and Georgia, legislators are considering asking women to sign a death warrant before they have an abortion. 'What they are doing is very clandestine,' says Julia Ernst of the Center for Reproductive Rights.

Table 3 – Abortion allowed?

25 per cent of the world's women live in countries where abortion is still illegal – or only legal if a woman's life is in danger.

Grounds on which abortion is legally permitted in 193 countries, 2001

	To save a woman's life	To preserve physical health	To preserve mental health	Rape or incest	Fetal impairment	Economic or social reasons	On request
All countries	**(193)**						
Permitted	189	122	120	83	76	63	52
Not permitted	4	71	73	110	117	130	141
Developed countries	**(48)**						
Permitted	46	42	41	39	39	36	31
Not permitted	2	6	7	9	9	12	17
Developing countries	**(145)**						
Permitted	143	80	79	44	37	27	21
Not permitted	2	65	66	101	108	118	124

Unsafe abortion. Global and regional estimates of the incidence of unsafe abortion and associated mortality in 2000, Fourth edition, World Health Organization, 2004.

'They are not doing a frontal assault. They are trying to fly under the radar screen, in part not to tip off the American public'. But it amounts to an outright attack on abortion – 'an assault on reproductive rights writ large,' says Ernst.[15] Between 1991 and 2005, state legislatures enacted 301 anti-abortion measures. Some people go even further. Groups like Operation Rescue have targeted – and even killed – people connected with abortion clinics.

The 'global gag' rule

In 2001, President Bush introduced a policy that disqualified non-governmental organizations (NGOs) outside the US from receiving US family planning funding if they provide legal abortion services (except in very narrow circumstances), counseling on termination, or lobby to make or keep abortion legal in their own country. The policy applies even if abortion is permitted locally, and even if organizations use non-US money.

Part of this policy included a decision to withhold $34 million in assistance to the UN Population Fund (UNFPA) on the grounds that its programs 'promote' abortion. On 13 September 2006, for the fifth time, Bush refused to release the money, leaving UNFPA with a total of $161 million in withheld funds.

Congressman Joseph Crowley is among those battling to get the funding reinstated: 'By withholding our contribution to UNFPA, we send a strong message to women in the developing world that we choose not to help.' In a protest letter to Bush, women's groups across the world said: 'We know that integrated sexual and reproductive health care saves lives, and that the single most effective strategy to prevent unnecessary deaths is to combine political will, economic resources, and sound public-health policies to strengthen and expand access to sexual and reproductive health services. Each and every one of these deaths can be

---

Effects of the global gag rule

The International Women's Health Coalition gives three specific examples of how the global gag rule affects women.

- 'Organizations cannot do any research to determine how many women die or are injured as a result of unsafe abortion in their countries, and cannot publicize those statistics.
- Even if abortion is legal (as it is in most countries in the world under certain circumstances), organizations are prohibited from giving women information about where they might obtain a safe, legal procedure.
- An organization that receives any funds from the US – which is the largest bilateral donor in many countries – faces what one local leader calls 'Sophie's Choice': The group must either knowingly withhold information and services from often desperate women, or risk losing what is often the bulk of its funding.'

prevented. Yet we watch as the US attempts on every level to undermine such services.'

In other countries, the right to abortion has been rescinded. In Nicaragua, for example, abortion was allowed for 'therapeutic reasons'. In November 2006, it was made completely illegal.

New technologies

The irony here is that although the last quarter of the 20th century saw many women still dying from illegal abortions, it also witnessed several major advances in reproductive medicine. One of the most controversial is the use of assisted reproductive technology (ART) to manage infertility. ART includes treatments like in-vitro fertilization (IVF) but also surrogacy (where a woman agrees to become pregnant and bear a child for a couple who often pay her) and the freezing of eggs and sperm.

Infertility affects more than 80 million people world-

Severe effects in Zambia

The 'global gag'* rule has severe consequences on the ground. In Zambia, for example, where abortion is legal, Planned Parenthood Federation of Zambia was the only organization in the country to refuse the terms of the gag rule. The consequences have been severe. It has lost nearly 40 per cent of its staff members, had to scale back services, and end community-based distribution of contraceptive supplies and health information. Financial losses caused by the gag rule have made it impossible to expand and have greatly hindered HIV-prevention efforts.

Smaller NGOs that depend on the Federation are struggling to keep their programs running and it can no longer share its resources with the government. In addition, many other organizations, afraid of the consequences of the global gag rule, have stopped informing women about emergency contraception. One staff member noted: 'We are worried about having to sign something that will force us to show that the money is not being used for any integrated programs. There was one NGO receiving US money which was going to give us funds... but then they wanted to make us sign onto the gag rule and promise that we wouldn't use the funds for certain things. This disturbed us.'[16]

* In 2001, President Bush introduced a policy that disqualified NGOs outside the US from receiving US family planning funding if they provide legal abortion services (except in very narrow circumstances).

---

wide, or one in 10 couples. Most of these live in the Majority World where infertility services in general, and ART in particular, are not available.[17]

Sexually transmitted diseases (STDs)

There are 340 million people who contract curable sexually transmitted diseases (excluding AIDS) each year.[18] One third of these are young people under 25. The consequences for women can be very serious and sometimes fatal (eg cervical cancer, ectopic pregnancy, sepsis, infertility). And yet women tend not to seek treatment – partly because the majority of such infections do not have any major symptoms, and partly because they fear the stigma attached to having such an infection, and may have neither time nor money for health care. In developing countries, STDs and their complications rank in the top five disease categories for which adults seek health care.

HIV/AIDS

Twenty years ago, HIV/AIDS was largely a male disease. But over the last few years, this has been slowly changing. Peter Piot, UNAIDS Executive Director, noted on World AIDS Day 2007 that 'the epidemic has globalized – and feminized. In 1988, most recorded cases of HIV were still in the United States, and most were among men. Today, HIV is present in every country in the world, and half those living with HIV are women.' The proportion varies from country to country. In sub-Saharan Africa, almost 60 per cent of adults living with HIV in 2007 were women, while in the Caribbean, Latin America, Asia and Eastern Europe the proportion of women is slowly growing.[19]

And when women die, their children are put at risk, even if they do not have the disease. For a girl, the death of her mother increases her own chances of dying by 400 per cent.

Table 4 – Women and HIV

In 1988 most cases were among men but today half of those living with HIV are women.

Percentage those living with HIV who are women, 2001-2007

	2007 % women	2001 % women
Global	50	50
Sub-Saharan Africa	60	61
Caribbean	43	27
Asia	29	26
E. Europe & Central Asia	26	23
Latin America	24	22

2007 AIDS epidemic update, UNAIDS/WHO http://data.unaids.org/pub/EPISlides/2007/2007_epiupdate_en.pd

So why have the numbers of women with HIV/AIDS increased so dramatically? Firstly, because their physiology makes them more vulnerable than men to HIV and other sexually transmitted diseases. Reproductive tract infections, which predispose to HIV infection, are more easily transmitted and less easy to diagnose in women. Vaginal cuts suffered during violent or coerced sex increase the risks.

Second, because women rarely have the power in a relationship to negotiate condom use, or prevent their husband or partner having relationships with others who may be infected.

Young women in particular are vulnerable. One study estimates that over half the world's population has had unprotected sex by age 16.[20] HIV-infection rates among young African women aged 15-19 in some urban areas are five to six times higher than for young men.

Mozambique's Prime Minister, Pascal Mocumbi, reported that the overall rate of infection among girls and young women in his country was twice that of boys their age: 'Not because the girls are promiscuous, but because nearly three out of five are married by age 18, 40 per cent of them to much older, sexually experienced men, who may expose their wives to HIV/AIDS. Abstinence is not an option for these child brides. Those who try to discuss condom use commonly face violence or rejection.'[21]

And yet in the US the Bush regime has consistently opposed sex education and argued for a focus on abstinence. A third of all prevention funds in the US Government's $15-billion Emergency Plan for AIDS Relief in Africa, the Caribbean and Vietnam are for abstinence-only programs. The International Women's Health Coalition notes that: 'Such programs fail to help young women whose husbands are HIV-positive, or young women forced to trade sex for food in order to survive. Unless prevention programs reflect the challenges and realities they face, HIV/AIDS rates among young people will continue to increase.'[22]

Responses that involve and treat young people – both men and women – and also deal with their relationships seem to be the best way of preventing HIV. This is why HIV-prevention programs are beginning to recognize that they need to target young men in particular, to provide them with information about prevention, to work on their self-respect, and respect for and dialogue with, young women, and to understand the particular pressures that they face, particularly where there are few job prospects and little to do.

'Around here there is only football, drink and sex. When it is dark there is only drink and sex. And when the drink runs out, there is sex,' said a young man from a rural area in Côte d'Ivoire.[23]

Until 1998 South Africa had one of the fastest expanding epidemics in the world, but HIV prevalence now appears to have stabilized, and may even be declining slightly. In one survey among young women, the rate fell from 15.9 per cent in 2005 to 13.7 per cent in 2006.[24] This suggests that awareness campaigns and prevention programs may be bearing fruit.

In Kenya, HIV prevalence among young pregnant women declined significantly by more than 25 per cent in both urban and rural areas, and there were similar

declines in urban areas of Côte d'Ivoire, Malawi and
Zimbabwe, and rural parts of Botswana.

Smaller declines have also occurred in both urban
and rural Burkina Faso, Namibia and Swaziland,
urban parts of the Bahamas, Botswana, Burundi and
Rwanda, and rural parts of Tanzania.

UNAIDS notes that: 'These behavior trends among
young people point to recent, encouraging changes in
some countries. For example, there have been striking
shifts in condom use during sex with non-regular partners. The proportion of young people who said they
used condoms the last time they had sex with a non-
regular partner increased for both men and women
in Cameroon, Haiti, Malawi and Tanzania, and for
women only in Côte d'Ivoire, Kenya, Togo, Rwanda
and Uganda.'[25]

Giving women the power to negotiate is crucial.
This comes both from education and from economic
security. A paper published in 2006 by the UNAIDS-
led Global Coalition on Women and AIDS (GCWA)
shows that when women have an income and a safe
place to live, they are much better able to negotiate
abstinence, fidelity, and safer sex.[26]

Occupational health

There are many steps between birth and death, and this
chapter has looked at only a few of the health issues
along that journey that relate particularly to women.
Occupational health is another important area; many
women's jobs still tend to be very different from men's
jobs and the health risks also vary. This sexual division
of labor affects women's health in six main ways:[27]

1 Women's jobs have specific characteristics (repetition,
monotony, static effort) which may lead over time to
changes in mental and physical health.
2 Spaces, equipment and schedules that are designed
for men may not be suitable for women.
3 Occupational segregation may result in health risks

for women and men by increasing monotony and repetition.

4 Sex-based job assignment may be vaunted as protecting the health of women and men and thus distract from more effective occupational health promotion practices.

5 Discrimination against women is stressful of itself and may affect women's mental health.

6 Part-time workers (mainly women) are often excluded from adequate sickness benefits, maternity pay, vacation pay and so on.

Mental health

More women than men suffer from mental health problems. Depression occurs two to three times more frequently in women than in men. The disparity in rates between the sexes tend to be even more pronounced in the developing world.[28] In addition, women living in poor social and environmental circumstances with associated low education, low income and difficult family and marital relationships, are much more likely than other women to suffer from mental disorders. Up to 20 per cent of those attending primary health care in developing countries suffer from anxiety and/or depressive disorders. In most centers, these patients are not recognized and therefore not treated.

Disease and death

The things that women die of are changing. Because illness related to child-bearing is such a serious problem in the Global South, it makes up three out of the ten leading causes of disease burden for women between 15 and 44 years old worldwide.

Tuberculosis (TB) has become the single biggest infectious killer of women today. 'Wives, mothers and wage earners are being cut down in their prime and the world isn't noticing,' said Dr Paul Dolin of WHO's Global Tuberculosis Programme. 'Yet the ripple effect on families, communities and economies will be felt

Birth and death

long after a woman has died.'

In the US, young women are developing 50 per cent more cancer than their grandmothers did. There has been a big increase in the number of deaths from breast cancer in the last 30 years, when one in 20 women died of the disease. Today the figure is one in eight. Breast cancer kills approximately 500,000 women each year, mostly in developed countries. Cervical cancer globally kills more than 250,000 women each year, with 80 per cent of these deaths occurring in developing countries.[29]

Deaths from breast cancer are related to access to medical care; in the US, for example, white women are more likely to get breast cancer, but black women are more likely to die from it. They are also related to environmental factors which increasingly affect our lives.

Breast cancer activists are increasingly certain that environmental factors, including exposure to plastics-based estrogen-mimicking chemicals, are responsible for the near-epidemic rates of the disease.[30] The relationship of women to the environment is the subject of Chapter 7.

1 www.who.int/making_pregnancy_safer/women_conference/speeches/en/ 2 *The Atlas of Women: an economic, social and political survey*, Joni Seager, Earthscan 2005. 3 www.who.int/mediacentre/news/releases/2007/pr56/en/ 4 *The State of the World's Mothers* 2004, Save the Children US. 5 www.unfpa.org/news/news.cfm?ID=154&Language=1 6 http://www.unicef-icdc.org/publications/pdf/repcard3e.pdf#search=%22teenage%20pregnancy%20unicef%22 7 *Birth rights: new approaches to Safe Motherhood*, Judy Mirsky, Panos Institute, 2001. 8 *The Atlas of Women*, Joni Seager, Earthscan 2005. 9 www.unfpa.org/rh/planning.htm 10 www.mountainvoices.org 11 *Attacking Poverty*, World Development Report 2000/2001. 12 United Nations Department of Public Information DPI/1772/HR–February 1996. 13 www.who.int/reproductive-health/publications/unsafeabortion_2003/ua_estimates03.pdf 14 www.unfpa.org/swp/1999/newsfeature3.htm 15 'When does life really begin?' Suzanne Goldenberg, *The Guardian*, 6 June 6 2003. 16 www.globalgagrule.org/caseStudy_zambia.htm 17 Current Practices and Controversies in Assisted Reproduction, www.who.int/reproductive-health 18 www.who.int/mediacentre/factsheets/fs110/en/index.html 19 data.unaids.org/pub/EPISlides/2007/071118_epi_regional%20factsheet_en.pdf 20 Policy paper on HIV/AIDS, Save the Children Fund [unpublished 2000]. 21 www.unaids.org/worldaidsday/2002/press/update/epiupdate2002/en.doc 22 www.iwhc.org/global/uspolicy/adolescents/index.cfm 23 *Young men and HIV: culture, poverty and sexual risk*, Thomas Scalway, Panos Institute/UNAIDS 2001. 24 www.avert.org/safricastats.htm 25 http://data.unaids.

org/pub/EPISlides/2007/2007_epiupdate_en.pdf **26** www.unaids.org/
en/KnowledgeCentre/Resources/FeatureStories/archive/2006/20060308-
economicsecurity.asp **27** www.who.int/oeh/OCHweb/OCHweb/OSHpages/
OSHDocuments/Women/ **28** World Bank, 1993. **29** www.who.int/features/
factfiles/women/10_en.html **30** *The Atlas of Women*, Joni Seager, Earthscan
2005.

3 Poverty, development and work

'Across the world, it is women who are driving economic growth. Over the last 30 years they have filled two out of every three new jobs.' CHERIE BOOTH, UK BARRISTER.[1]

Women make up the majority of the world's poor people. The gap between women and men caught in the cycle of poverty has continued to widen, a phenomenon commonly referred to as 'the feminization of poverty'.

WOMEN LIVING IN poverty are often denied access to critical resources such as credit, land and inheritance. Their labor goes unrewarded and unrecognized. Their health care and nutritional needs are not given priority, they lack sufficient access to education and support services, and their participation in decision-making at home and in the community are minimal. And often they lack the resources and services to change their situation.

This should have changed. 'Development' in the last 15 years has seen a major focus on 'gender'. Donors have said they will not fund projects unless there is a gender dimension, and any application has to explain what this is. 'No poverty reduction strategy in Least Developed Countries could be successful without creation of productive employment with special attention to women and the youth,' said Anwarul K Chowdhury, the UN Under-Secretary-General.[2]

There are gender budgets and gender mainstreaming, and all development has to be viewed through a 'gender lens'. This shift of focus from women to gender in theory meant that rather than concentrating on women alone, the focus was on the complex network of social, political and economic relationships between men and women, with a view to improving the lives of all. In practice, however, there is much confusion about what gender means and in some cases resistance from men. Has this improved the lives of women? There seems little evidence that this is the case. One of the interesting facts noted by *Social Watch* in the introduction to its statistics on gender equality is that 'a country's level of wealth does not automatically determine its degree of equity.' It cites Rwanda, one of the world's least developed countries, which ranks third on the Gender Equality Index, thanks to a number of affirmative actions, not least in the area of getting women into parliament. The Index also notes that there has been 'either very slow progress or no progress at all', and that the US is one of the countries that have experienced the greatest regression in women's rights. It concluded: 'Obviously, the key to gender equity lies not in a country's economic power, but rather in its government's political will.'[3]

There have been many commitments to improving the lives of poor women, not least the Beijing Platform for Action, signed by 189 countries, which recognizes the crucial link between gender equality and poverty eradication. In 2000, the Millennium Development Goals recommitted those governments to the eradication of poverty and to equality between men and women.

But in fact, aid money directed at women is falling. Between 2002 and 2003, the percentage of aid money targeting women or supporting women's organizations fell from 0.23 per cent to 0.136 per cent.[4] A 2006 study of funding for women's rights organizations found that 31 per cent reported receiving less funding in 2005 than in 2000, and this was true for traditional funding sources, like bi- and multilateral donors, as well as from private and public foundations.[5] The report noted that 'despite growing public awareness of the centrality of gender equality and women's rights in development, funding for the protection and guarantee of the rights of

Poverty, development and work

Table 5 – Women's places

Rwanda has a good ranking for improvement in equality for women, while the US is near the bottom of the pile of those which are back-sliding.

Gender Equality Index (GEI), top and bottom 10 countries, 2007

The 10 countries with the greatest GEI progress

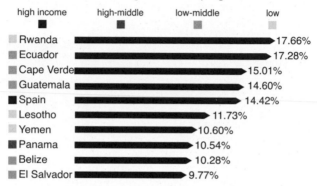

Measuring variation as a precentage, the countries that registered most progress during this period were: in the first place Rwanda, followed by Ecuador, Cape Verde and Guatemala

The 10 countries with the greatest GEI regression

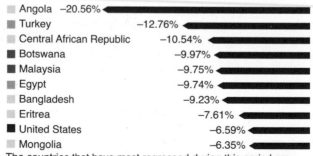

The countries that have most regressed during this period are Angola (21%) and Turkey (13%). Amongst the 10 countries that most regressed are ones with a low, low-middle, high-middle and high income, for example in the latter category, the United States.

www.socialwatch.org/en/avancesyRetrocesos/IEG/tablas/GEIvalues2007.htm

Gender is a bad thing

'Gender is a bad thing. Especially when you see these women on TV who talk like men and who are very argumentative. We have one woman like that in this organization... But my secretary is different. She is like my wife. She makes sure my hair is combed and my tie is straight. She also makes me tea, sometimes she types my love letters and she also does the office filing.' Emmanuel, NGO director, Zambia.

A report based on research in four countries in Africa found that there was great confusion about what 'gender' meant. By some, it was seen as an external and imported concept, divorced from peoples, own analysis and understanding of gender in their communities and organizations.

- Men, and many women, felt alienated by the rather confrontational approach taken, and as a result many were hostile to the messages of gender equity.
- Gender equity was understood simply as the need for numerical balance in society, called '50:50'. People had a poor grasp of why 50:50 was important and the accompanying idea that women and men can all do each other's work equally was a source of ridicule in many communities.
- Non-governmental organizations ostensibly subscribed to these gender concepts, but many were found to be skeptical and were just repeating the terms in order to access donor funding, or 'masquerading' – pretending to understand and support new gender terminology and concepts while rejecting them because they clashed with their own beliefs or position in society. Only a few 'gender embracers' were found, who were committed to addressing gender inequalities in their organizations and communities.
- 'Masqueraders' took gender training and exhortations into communities, but left these behind within their own family and organizational lives.

Living Gender in African Organizations and Communities: Stories from The Gambia, Rwanda, Uganda and Zambia, Senorina Wendoh and Tina Wallace, May 2006, Transform Africa
www.transformafrica.org/docs/gender_research_report.pdf

women continues to be grossly insufficient.' The latest aid agreement, the Paris Declaration, does not mention gender equality until page 42 of the 50-page document, except for a reference to it as a 'cross-cutting issue'. There are many reasons for this. The security agendas since the attacks of 11 September 2001: the consolidation of funds towards larger organizations, increasingly stringent accounting procedures from funders, the failure of the gender mainstreaming agenda, lack of accountability and the impact of the security agenda and 'war against terror' (see box p. 47).

Paid work
Much of women's work remains unrecognized, uncounted and unpaid; in the home, in agriculture, in food production and in childcare. Globalization has brought one main benefit to many women: more paid work. Since 1980, the growth in women's labor force has been substantially higher than that of men in every region of the world except Africa (where the two labor forces have grown at the same rate). In Latin America the growth rate for women has been more than three times as great as that of men, at an annual average of over four per cent, while in the European Union 80 per cent of all labor force growth is attributed to women's increasing participation.[6] Professor Saud Choudhury of Canada's Trent University notes: 'The economic independence that these jobs provide has for the first time given Third World women the ability to contribute to their families financially; the opportunity to delay marriages and child-bearing; even the means to end oppressive marital relationships.'[7]

In the last decade since 1996, however, the numbers of women in the workforce have slightly declined, due in part to the fact that more young women are in education and therefore not working.[8] The largest gaps in the female and male labor force participation rates were in the Middle East, North Africa and South Asia.

And while more women may be working, they are still paid less than men. In the US in 2003, on average, women earned 75.5 per cent of men's wages. This was down for the first time in four years.[9] And that number falls to 67 per cent for African-American women and 56 per cent for Latinas.[10] The pay gap is actually worse at the top of the scale: in Britain in 2007, the only two women heading any of the top 100 companies had salaries respectively 75 and 25 per cent behind the average paid to their male counterparts. There were 16 women executives at the top level in 2007 – four more than 12 months earlier but still a tiny fraction of a total of 527.[11] In the US, in 2005, unversity-educated women between 36 and 45 years old earned 74.7 cents for every dollar earned by a man in the same group. A decade earlier, the figure was 75.7 cents.[12]

In addition, women are often assigned to the worst-paid, short-contract, most monotonous jobs in order to make ends meet. In the 1990s, the numbers of women part-timers increased in most industrialized countries, where on average women make up three-quarters of all part-time workers. In some EU countries, such as Austria, Germany and Luxembourg, women make up more than 85 per cent of part-time workers.[13]

In addition, there has been an increase in 'permanent

Poverty vs security?

Since the attacks of 11 September 2001, security agendas, driven by the United States, have overwhelmed the foreign policies of many donor governments... a very large portion of the increase of ODA [overseas development assistance] in 2005 was for so-called military reconstruction projects in Iraq and Afghanistan that are currently counted in foreign aid budgets. That said, ODA costs are minute in proportion to military spending given the fact that the US Government alone is now spending nearly $10 billion a month in Iraq and Afghanistan. According to the *Reality of Aid* report, the US spends 76 times more on the war in Iraq than its total ODA for health, 196 times more compared to education and 480 times what it allocates to water and sanitation worldwide.

The impact of the security agenda on foreign development assistance has made poverty eradication a lower priority: foreign policy related to the donors' 'war on terror' is where the funds are flowing. And so while this should in theory mean funds for women's rights organizations in Afghanistan and Iraq, especially given the doctrines of the US alongside several Western governments to fight against Islamic extremists for 'democracy and women's emancipation', this has not been the case. Women's organizations in Iraq and Afghanistan have had to struggle for resources that most often get absorbed by international non-governmental organizations or multilateral agencies.

www.awid.org/publications/fundher_2/chapter3.pdf

Raw deal for women in Britain
- Women working full-time earn, on average, 17 per cent less an hour than men working full-time. For women working part-time the gap is 36 per cent an hour.
- Two-fifths of women in employment in Britain work part-time, compared with 11 per cent of men.
- Only 11 per cent of directors of the UK's top 100 companies are women, although the number of women in non-executive positions increased in 2007 to 110 from 102 in 2006.
- The number of women holding executive positions in FTSE 100 companies in 2007 fell to the lowest level for nine years.

www.fawcettsociety.org.uk and 'Why women in business become the solution, not the problem', *The Guardian*, 5 February 2008.

---

temporary employment' where workers exist on a series of short-term contracts. Such employment is directed mainly at women and other discriminated-against groups. But their incorporation into global markets in this way has given them little security, few benefits, and no negotiating power. Such jobs are also vulnerable to external economic crises – it is estimated that during the collapse of the south and east Asian economies in 1998,

---

No choice, no voice
- In Morocco, women in one Tangier garment factory put in around 90 hours of overtime in July 2003. But according to their employer, the extra hours were simply part of the workers' obligation to meet their targets, so did not count as official overtime. At the end of the month the women received only 50 to 60 per cent of their rightful earnings as a result.
- Tomato-pickers in Florida, US, put in 148 hours of overtime work each month in the picking season. But since they are paid piece-rate, overtime pay doesn't exist. As a result, they earn between 50 and 80 per cent of what a long-term employee would earn for the same hours.
- Garment-workers from seven factories in Bangladesh interviewed in 2003 worked on average 80 hours of overtime per month. Not one received a payslip. They were paid between 60 and 80 per cent of their due earnings – on average, the equivalent of doing 24 hours of unpaid work a month.

'Trading away our rights: women working in global supply chains', Oxfam GB 2004, www.oxfam.org

---

10,000 workers, most of them women, were laid off every day in South Korea, while others faced reductions of up to 100 per cent in their wage packets.[14] 'This was inevitable,' comments the UN's Economic and Social Commission for Asia and the Pacific, 'given that women were originally preferred as workers largely because of the greater ease of dismissal.'

Victoria Tauli-Corpuz, director of the Tebtebba Foundation in the Philippines, adds: 'Although global-ization resulted in some women gaining employment in the manufacturing sector, the majority of Asian women are still found in the informal economy, rural farming communities, and in subsistence economic activities. The shifts in production patterns due to globalization... have led to the dislocation of women from their traditional sources of livelihood.'[15]

Women in Export Processing Zones

Around 70 to 90 per cent of the 43 million people working in the world's 5,000 export processing zones (EPZs) are women.[16] EPZs have particular economic advantages which attract foreign investment. They produce textiles, sporting goods, electronics and foot-wear, often for Northern markets. Pay levels for workers are often higher than outside the zone, but workers often have long hours, limited job security,

Table 6 – Women and work

In Colombia, Kenya and Zimbabwe women's work is mostly in agriculture while in the other countries below it is mainly garment work in factories.

Women as a percentage of production employees

	%
Bangladesh	85
Cambodia	90
Colombia	65
Honduras	65
Kenya	75
Morocco	70
Zimbabwe	87

C Dolan, and K Sorby (2003) and Oxfam research reports, quoted in 'Trading away our rights: women working in global supply chains', Oxfam GB, 2004 www.oxfam.org

---

The effects of globalization on women

- In Chile, 75 per cent of women in the agricultural sector are hired on temporary contracts picking fruit, and put in more than 60 hours a week during the season. But one in three still earns below the minimum wage.
- Fewer than half of the women employed in Bangladesh's textile and garment export sector have a contract, and the vast majority gets no maternity or health coverage – but 80 per cent fear dismissal if they complain.
- In China's Guangdong province, one of the world's fastest growing industrial areas, young women face 150 hours of overtime each month in the garment factories – but 60 per cent have no written contract and 90 per cent have no access to social insurance.

'Trading away our rights: women working in global supply chains', Oxfam GB 2004, www.oxfam.org

---

and few opportunities for training or advancement. In many EPZs – for example, in Bangladesh, Pakistan and Zimbabwe – trade unions are banned. Their advantages for women are questionable, as the story from Kenya illustrates (see box p. 51).

Vivian Stromberg, Executive Director of Madre, a US organization working with some of the world's poorest women, said: 'In our experience with recently opened markets, women are virtual prisoners in many factories, subject to physical violence including sexual assault, strip searches, attacks on union organizers, and forced consumption of amphetamines to increase output. Women work longer hours than their male counterparts, are paid half the wages, and suffer from serious work-related health problems, including lung damage, memory loss and numbness from exposure to toxic materials.'[17]

While the spread of global markets may have helped some sectors of the population in the Majority World, and created jobs (though not necessarily the kind of jobs that women want) it is likely to have made things worse for those at the bottom of the heap. And these are mostly women.

Lucy's story

Lucy, a Kenyan mother of two, sews the pockets onto children's jeans destined for Wal-Mart in the United States, the world's most successful retailer. Her factory, based in an export processing zone (EPZ) outside Nairobi, receives erratic, sub-contracted orders and must keep costs low and output high. Early in 2003, when her manager demanded she work non-stop for two days and nights to meet the shipping deadline, her partner walked out, leaving Lucy to raise the children, aged two and 13. 'He said he will come back when the condition of my work is good,' she said, 'Till today the condition is becoming worse.'

In May Lucy sold her table, cupboard, and bed so that she could pay the rent. Then she sold the cooking stove to buy her son's school uniform. In June, when orders stopped for eight weeks, so did the pay. Her parents, living in a village 90 miles/150 kilometers north of Nairobi, agreed to take her children, and she has not seen them for six months. 'If this EPZ could be better, and consider us as people, and give us leave and holidays, then I would be able to go and see the children,' she said.

Production targets are unrealistically high, and Lucy is expected to put in extra hours to meet them. In September she worked 20 hours of overtime but was paid for only six.

Talk of trade unions is banned, and the factory atmosphere is intimidating. 'Supervisors abuse us... If we talk, they say, "Shut your beak. Even a child can do your job."' She most pities the young female helpers doing the low-skill tasks such as counting and cleaning the garments. 'If you are a helper, you need security,' she said. 'They are sexually harassed to keep their job. That's why as women we are so oppressed. Because you can't secure your job through the trade union, you have to buy it with sex.'

Lucy depends on this job. But she and her family should not be forced to pay such a price to keep it. Worldwide, working women like her – making garments, cutting flowers and picking fruit – are demanding their fair share of the gains from trade. The only asset they have to offer in trade is their labor. This makes a critical test for globalization: Can it create jobs that empower, rather than undermine, women as workers? So far it is failing.'

'Trading away our rights: women working in global supply chains', Oxfam GB 2004, www.oxfam.org

Wired women

Most of us could not imagine life without the internet. But 80 per cent of users are in the industrialized world, and the majority of users are men. This is slowly changing as more women find the internet a useful tool and access to cybercafes makes it possible. In Russia for example, 38 per cent of internet users are female, in India, 23 per cent, in China 30 per cent, in Brazil 40 per cent and in South Africa 49 per cent.[18]

Migration and trafficking of women
The lifting of restrictions on the movement of people across borders, brought about by globalization, has meant that women can move around more independently than ever before. Migration can provide women with new opportunities, financial independence and status in their home country. Almost 50 per cent of the world's 191 million migrants are women. In some regions this number is even higher.[19] Women migrants often send more money home than their male counterparts. 'The money that female migrants send home can raise families and even entire communities out of poverty,' says the United Nations.[20] In their host countries, they have many skills to bring but are still often considered second-class citizens.

In Asia, women are now the majority of expatriates working abroad. This has been a big change over the last 20 years, when migrants were mainly men. In Sri Lanka, between 1986 and 1999, female migrant workers increased from 33 per cent to 65 per cent

---

At the click of a button
The internet is beginning to have a revolutionary effect on the 700 million people who live in villages in India – and the change is being led by women. A project set up by one of India's leading technology institutes has put women in charge of forging the way across the digital divide as the proprietors of a fast-growing number of internet cafes or kiosks around the sub-continent. In total 80 per cent of these new kiosks are run by women, many of whom have had very little or no acquaintance with technology before.

Asha Sanjay, of the Indian Institute of Technology (IIT) in Chennai (Madras) that established the scheme, says that while in some places people are not able to get a bus to the next village, the net allows them to connect to the world. 'Here they can do it at the click of a button,' she told BBC World Service's Everywoman program, 'It's really something.'

http://news.bbc.co.uk

of the total migrant workforce. In 1999, remittances from Sri Lankan female migrant workers accounted for 50 per cent of the country's trade balance and 145 per cent of gross foreign loans and grants. Women accounted for 70 per cent of migrant workers abroad in the Philippines in 2000. Most traveled alone and were the main providers for their families back home. Filipino women migrants contributed $6.2 billion in total remittances for 2001.[21]

But, says the International Organization for Migration (IOM), 'women migrants are more exposed to forced labor, sexual exploitation and violence than men and are also more likely to accept precarious working conditions and lower wages.'

Globalization has also contributed to a worldwide growth in the numbers of women and girls being trafficked for forced sexual services. The International Labour Organization (ILO) estimates that $28 billion year is made from the sexual exploitation of women and children. One report notes that: 'The sale of people into trafficking is thought to be the third largest and the fastest-growing, criminal activity in the world, behind arms and drugs trafficking.'[22] Between 700,000 and two million women are involved every year, a large proportion of whom are sold many times over. Some 80 per cent of those being trafficked globally are girls and women and up to half are children.[23]

Economic crises and disparities between countries fuel supply, while economic liberalization has led to a demand for cheap labor. Where economic growth has meant an expanding middle class – as in Indonesia, Malaysia and the Philippines – men have more money to buy sexual services. In other countries, widespread poverty has meant that women are lured by the promise of a good job in another country – though few know what they face when they arrive. Traffickers exploit women's desire to make a better life for themselves with promises of jobs as waitresses, dancers, models, maids and nannies. Once they arrive, their passports are taken away and they are forced to work as prostitutes. And even if they manage to escape, their families will often not have them back as they have been 'dishonored'.

'Nothing else to lose'

The advert that changed her life was brief. 'Girls and women under 35. Well paid jobs abroad.' Olga and her friend Vica saw this ad in a local newspaper, and thought they'd found a fantastic opportunity. They called the contact number and met a Moldovan man who told them they would be employed as healthcare auxiliaries in Milan, earning $1,000 a month each. This was a staggering offer for the two young women. When he asked how soon they could start work, Olga and Vica both agreed to leave Chisinau a week later.

Olga and Vica left Chisinau on a minibus with eight other Moldovan women who believed they were going to Italy too. After crossing the border to Romania they drove on narrow country roads avoiding towns and cities. Olga was already uneasy. She had been given a fake passport at the border and instinctively knew something was wrong: but she was intimidated and, like the others, said nothing. They were all constantly watched. After several days they crossed the Danube River to Serbia, and their journey continued overland until they were instructed to walk through a forest at night, following a guide. When they emerged from the trees they were told they were in Kosovo.

'We were all taken to a bar,' says Olga quietly. 'We were told we owed a lot of money for our journey and we had to work to pay it back. Some of the women were auctioned in the middle of the bar and taken away. The rest of us were kept there and ordered to start work.'

After almost two years of abuse another trafficked woman helped her hide in a cupboard and then flee when the bar owner left the premises. She fled to a local police station and was taken into protective custody. When I asked what had prompted her escape, this is what she told me. 'If I had stayed at that place any longer I would have been blind. I had no choice. He was beating me in my head and in my eyes.'

Olga returned to Moldova with the International Organization for Migration (IOM) and then flew to Kiev, for eye surgery. The surgeons did all they could to repair her detached retinas, but she is still almost blind. She survives on a small state disability pension. When I met her, she insisted I tell her story using her real name.

'I have nothing else to lose,' she said. 'I have survived but I am not the same person that I was.'

'Use my name', by Louisa Waugh, in 'Trafficked for sexual exploitation', *New Internationalist* 404, September 2007.

Chapter 5 looks at how women have been able to use newly acquired legal rights to change their situation at international, national and local levels.

1 *The Observer*, 28 January 2007. 2 www.un.org/apps/news/story. asp?NewsID=16557&Cr=least&Cr1=develop 3 www.socialwatch.org/en/ avancesyRetrocesos/IEG/index.htm 4 *Social Watch*, February 2005: 22. 5 www.ccic.ca/e/docs/003_acf_2007-10_gender_and_aid_effectiveness. pdf 6 *Globalization and employment: new opportunities, real threats*, Panos briefing 33, May 1999. 7 'Women Workers in the Global Factory: Impact of Gender Power Asymmetries', Saud Choudhury, in *The Political Economy of Globalization*, quoted in Panos briefing 33 *above*. 8 www.ilo. org/public/english/employment/strat/kilm/download/exsum.pdf 9 www. usatoday.com/money/workplace/2004-08-26-women_x.htm 10 www. guardian.co.uk/uselections08/story/0,,2027944,00.html 11 www.guardian. co.uk/business/2007/aug/29/executivepay.money 12 www.iht.com/ articles/2006/12/25/business/gender.php?page=3 13 www.ilo.org/public/ english/employment/strat/kilm/download/kilm05.pdf 14 *Globalisation and employment: new opportunities, real threats*, Panos briefing 33, May 1999. 15 'Asia-Pacific women grapple with financial crisis and globalization', Victoria Tauli-Corpuz, *Third World Resurgence*, no 94 (June 1998). 16 www.labour-inspection.org/EPZ.experiences.tradeunionpoint.htm 17 www. madre.org/art_manyfaces.html 18 *The Atlas of Women in the World*, Joni Seager, Earthscan 2005 19 www.iom.int/jahia/Jahia/pid/254 20 www.ft.com/cms/s/0/7727209a-3d8c-11db-bd60-0000779e2340.html 21 hwww.iom.int/en/news/pr858_en.shtml 22 Heather Montogmery, Zosa de Sas Kropiwnicki and Roz Evans, 'Trafficking women and children: overcoming the illegal sex trade' Refugee Studies Centre, Oxford, 2005. 23 www.unicef. org/protection/index_childlabour.html

4 Blogging and shopping: woman as global consumer

'Globalization has had a mixed impact on women's rights. On the one hand, it has led to increasing violations of women's economic, political, and cultural rights... On the other hand, aspects of globalization have provided women with increasing opportunities... to demand their rights.' UNESCO[1]

Globalization has changed the face of our world, making us all into global consumers and giving us access to instant information. This has affected women both negatively and positively.

WHEN THE PEOPLE of the future look back on our century and the last, globalization is likely to be seen as its defining feature: people traveling around the world; instant communication between continents; the spread of free trade, and the rise of a global consumer culture. 'The process in which economic, financial, technical and cultural transactions between different countries and communities around the world are increasingly interconnected, and embody common elements of experience, practice and understanding,' as one definition puts it.[2]

In this chapter we will be looking at how globalization has affected women in particular; both in terms of the spread of culture, consumerism and communications technologies, and also how the effects of other technologies affect women's lives.

The global consumer

For those who have money, globalization has led to a world in which choice is king and the consumer is the champion. In a world where, as former British Prime Minister Margaret Thatcher once famously said, 'there is no such thing as society', everyone has become an individual, a 'consumer', someone to be marketed at. An increasingly consumerist culture sees shopping, not politics or rights, as the solution to our woes – more young people in the UK voted on the television show 'Big Brother' than voted in the last election. And the ways that women have been targeted, and used for marketing, have changed considerably in the last decade.

Using women's bodies in advertising, for example, has become commonplace. Super-models and celebrities are the new role models for women and they are also super-thin, promoting an image of the 'perfect shape' that few can aspire to.

Increasing numbers are opting for cosmetic surgery in order to pursue the illusion of youth and beauty. Cosmetic surgery is being used by younger and younger women. 'A girl ought to have the right to decide whether she wants breast implants if she is an otherwise normal 16-year-old with little breast

---

Fat stats

- 42 per cent of 1st-3rd grade girls (under the age of 10) want to be thinner.
- 81 per cent of 10-year-olds are afraid of being fat.
- The average American woman is 5'4" tall and weighs 140 pounds/63 kg. The average American model is 5'11" tall and weighs 117 pounds/53 kg.
- Most fashion models are thinner than 98 per cent of American women.
- 46 per cent of 9-11 year-olds are 'sometimes' or 'very often' on diets, and 82 per cent* of their families are 'sometimes' or 'very often' on diets.
- 91 per cent of women recently surveyed on a college campus had attempted to control their weight through dieting, 22 per cent dieted 'often' or 'always'.
- Americans spend over $40 billion on dieting and diet-related products each year.

* *Branded: the buying and selling of teenagers*, Alissa Quart, Arrow 2003.
www.geocities.com/youth4sa/advertising.html

Blogging and shopping

www.plasticsurgery.org

Table 7 – Body beautiful?

Cosmetic surgery has increased hugely in the last ten years. In 2006, women had 11 million cosmetic procedures and 9.1 million 'minimally-invasive cosmetic procedures' such as Botox injections.

Cosmetic surgery in the US

	1992	2000	2006
Breast augmentation	32,607	291,350	329,396
Breast lift	n/a	52,846	103,788
Liposuction	47,212	354,015	302,789
Nose reshaping	50,175	389,155	307,258
Eyelid surgery	59,461	327,514	233,200
Facelift	40,077	133,856	104,055
Tummy tuck	n/a	62,713	146,240
Total	–	229,532	1,852,012

development,' says Paul Weiss, a member of the American Society of Plastic Surgeons.

'It is totally common for people to have their eyes done, their chins implanted, their ears pinned back,' says Mara, aged 17, from New York City Women's College. Plastic surgery is more and more accepted, and people do it either in 5th grade or after high school, before college.'[3] In one year in the US, the number of cosmetic operations on girls aged under 18 jumped 21.8 per cent, from 65,231 to 79,501.[4] Surgery can cost up to $7,000 and many girls work and go into debt in order to afford the operation that they think will change their lives.

This desire to look 'perfect' also affects young women's eating habits. More than half of teenage girls are, or think they should be, on a diet. In a 1998 survey by Exeter University in Britain, 57.5 per cent of 37,500 girls aged between 12 and 15 listed 'appearance' as the biggest concern in their lives.

In the US, anorexia – defined as 'the relentless pursuit of thinness' – affects one out of every hundred young women and some have literally starved themselves to death. Bulimia, where women binge eat and then make themselves sick, affects four in every hundred. Ninety per cent of people with these disorders are female. Most are in their teens and twenties.

Women and technology

New technologies are an inextricable part of globalization and are in the business of transforming people's lives. Whether in production, agricultural or otherwise, or reproduction, or transportation, they also have gender distinctions (in terms of access, use, benefits) and have the potential to make women's lives better – or worse.

For example, ever since Dolly the sheep was cloned in 1997, there has been considerable debate – and some unusual alliances – between those in favor of cloning and gene transplantation technologies, and those against. Cloning involves taking an egg from a female and using it to create another being identical in its DNA to the first. Gene transplantation techniques involve the selection of certain genes for a fetus.

Because women bear children, women's organizations have been in the forefront of these discussions. For financial reasons, cloning experiments are done within the corporate sector, by researchers who work either for biotechnology companies or in university laboratories with significant personal, departmental, or institutional financial stakes in the success of commercial biotech enterprises.

Women's groups say that such technologies would 'move decisions about reproduction further away from women, not only toward doctors and technicians but also toward marketers proffering the "enhancements" developed by biotech companies.'

They say that women may find themselves losing more and more control over childbearing, and under pressure to do all they can to produce the 'perfect baby'.[5]

Disability rights activists note that prenatal screening already makes it possible for women to abort babies who are not considered 'perfect' or to choose male over female babies. These developments, they say, would put women in the position of 'eugenic gatekeepers', able to choose not only whether to have a certain baby or not but, eventually, whether that baby would have blue eyes or brown, be short or tall, good-looking and intelligent. Even if this were desirable, what of the many parents who could not afford to have their children genetically enhanced in this way?

At present, cloning is still a dangerous business. And fundamental questions remain, not least of which is: in a market economy, who would decide what was on offer to whom?[6]

Information technology

Girl talk

The rise in social networking sites such as Facebook, MySpace and Bebo has also led to an increase in women using the web. In the UK, women aged between 25 and 49 are now spending more time on the internet than men, according to research by UK telecoms regulator Ofcom. These sites are visited by more than six million Britons each month.

James Thickett, director of research with Ofcom, said: 'Young women are finally finding content relevant to them on the internet. Social networking is what is driving a lot of usage; websites like Facebook and Bebo have a much higher female profile.'

Forrester Research, the technology specialist, describes the net as just another channel for women to do what they enjoy: 'shopping, talking, and caring'. Its data, based on research of young people across Europe, shows that 55 per cent of women aged 18 to 34 – or 4.13 million – use the medium regularly compared with 45 per cent – or 3.49 million – of men. Women are also likely to spend more time on networking sites when they are there.

Sharon Bailey, general manager for MSN, Microsoft's online business, said that 78 per cent of the users on the company's health and wellbeing site were women.

She said: 'If learning how to use the technology was ever a barrier to women getting online, it isn't today and, frankly, there are more interesting things for women to do on the web than in the past – especially when it comes to socializing.'

However, older men are still more prolific users of the internet than older women. Of those aged over 65, men account for 79 per cent of the overall time spent online.

http://technology.timesonline.co.uk/tol/news/tech_and_web/article2310548.ece

Blogging for Feminism

As we have seen in chapter one, young women are adopting a whole new attitude to feminism. A number of young women have set up feminist websites. Amanda Marcotte, blogger for Pandagon.net, says that 'the awesome thing about blogs is that they tear down so many of the obstacles that make it hard for an individual woman's stories to get an audience. The personal touch makes blogging a fertile ground for doing the hard work of waking people up to sexism and getting them committed to fighting it.'

Full Frontal Feminism: A Young Woman's Guide to Why Feminism Matters, Jessica Valenti, Seal Press, 2007.

Women still lag behind men in most countries in their use of information technology. While they make up 42 per cent of all internet users globally, this ranges from almost nothing in some countries to over 50 per cent in Canada and the US.[7] Seventy-nine per cent of internet users are in the rich world.

However, globally, there are some fundamental problems to increasing women's access – in Africa, for example, rural women are predominantly illiterate. One study in Guinea-Bissau showed that 74 per cent of women were illiterate.[8] However, the same survey showed that 92 per cent of women believed access to the internet to be crucial to women's development. 'Unless African women can participate fully in cyberspace, they will face a new form of exclusion from society,' says Marie-Helene Mottin-Sylla of the Synergy, Gender and Development Program of the NGO, ENDA Tiers Monde, in Senegal.[9] Ease of communication has also meant many internet-based jobs being among those moved to the South. This brings work to women in Bangalore or Barbados, but it also begs many questions.

What is not in doubt is that connection brings many benefits for women. Fadia Faqir, the coordinator for the Center of Middle Eastern Women Studies at Durham University in England says: 'Women in Jordan have access to the internet and 45 satellite channels,

Blogging and shopping

Table 8 – Mybook is YourSpace

While many women, especially young women, are racing to get online, others find it more difficult.

Why some women don't use communications technology

	%
Awareness of ICTs*	69
Literacy levels	68
Awareness of potential of ICT	65
Lack of ICT skills	60
Cost of access to telecommunications	59
Language	54
Time availability	44

*information and communications technologies (ICTs)

and because of that exposure, have aspirations that they can change their lives. If you can look in your neighbor's garden and you see an alternative, you start thinking of alternatives for yourself.'

The internet also makes global campaigning possible – for example, the Asia Monitor Research Centre joined forces with the London-based World Development Movement, the British Trades Union Congress and other groups across Europe to achieve better conditions for workers in Asia's toy-producing factories.

The 2003 World Summit on the Information Society aimed to examine the information revolution and its impact on people's lives. But its declaration of principles has been criticized by women's groups because it 'does not explicitly confront the fact that fundamental political, social and economic inequalities shape our world' and does not 'adequately recognize the centrality of gender inequality to broader social inequality.'[10]

Since then, there appear to have been few global surveys looking at the number of women online. The 2006 Information and Communications for Development Report from the World Bank on Global Trends and Policies only mentions women once on page 47 and gender on page 48. The most recent statistics on female internet use are from 2002, and show that while in the US and Canada more women than men use the web, in other countries the proportion is still low. Bearing in mind that the internet continues to be dominated by users in the rich world, in 2006, less than five out of every 100 Africans used the internet, compared with a rich world average of one out of every two – so in some countries this means very few women. In others, statistics are not monitored by gender. But in some places, increasing numbers of women are beginning to use the internet, although in general it is still dominated by men outside the rich world. In China, for example, the proportion of female home internet users is growing, especially in the main cities, but men still outnumber women three to two in internet use.[11]

New authority

One of the positive aspects of globalization has been the thousands of women's organizations that have emerged over the last 20 years campaigning on a wide range of different development issues, from HIV/AIDs to environment, political representation to poverty. This has given many women a new authority with which to counter some of the negative effects of the globalization process.

1 http://portal.unesco.org/shs/en/ev.php-URL_ID=7702&URL_DO=DO_TOPIC&URL_SECTION=201.html **2** 'Moving the goalposts: gender and globalization in the twenty-first century' *Gender and Development* vol 8 (1) R Pearson, 2000. **3** *Branded: the buying and selling of teenagers,* Alissa Quart, Arrow 2003. **4** ibid. **5** Council for responsible genetics, article by Marcy Darnovsky, www.gene-watch.org/genewatch/articles/14-4germline-women.html **6** See www.puaf.umd.edu/IPPP/Fall97Report/cloning.htm and www.gene-watch.org/genewatch/ articles/14-4germlinewomen.html **7** www.itu.com **8** www.idrc.ca/acacia/outputs/womenicts.html#Introduction **9** *The Internet and Poverty, Real Help or real Hype?* Panos 1998. **10** The Association for Progressive Communication (APC) Women's Programme. **11** http://www.internetworldstats.com/articles/art045.htm

5 Power, politics and the law

'The 21st century is ours, no doubt. I don't think even in a machista country like Brazil, being a woman today is something that goes against you.' MARTA SUPLICY, FORMER MAYOR OF SÃO PAULO AND NOW MINISTER OF TOURISM.[1]

There are more women in politics than ever before, though actual numbers are still small. And this is beginning to have an effect on legislation about women's rights.

SINCE THE LAST edition of this book, there has been a slow increase in the number of women leaders. By mid-2008, there were six female presidents – in Argentina, Chile, Finland, India, Ireland, Liberia and the Philippines and six women Prime Ministers – Germany, New Zealand, Mozambique, Netherlands Antilles, Ukraine and the Åland Islands (autonomous state). Many have been elected only in the last few years. By the end of the year there may be the first woman President in the White House. While having a woman in charge does not necessarily mean that things get better for ordinary women, at the very least it shows that women are capable of high office. And some women presidents are really committed to making a difference for other women – see the box on Ellen Johnson-Sirleaf (p. 65).

This gradual change – and six out of 192 countries of the United Nations is still a small proportion – is significant. At the same time, women have been slowly acquiring a greater share of seats in parliament. This revolution has happened mainly where special measures have been taken to increase numbers, as in Mozambique, where women now hold 34.8 per cent of the seats. They are not related to the relative 'development' of a country – at 16.3 per cent, the US has a lower share of women in power than many

Ellen Johnson-Sirleaf

In 2005, Ellen Johnson-Sirleaf became Africa's first elected female head of state when she became President of Liberia. She had been a public figure for many years. She was imprisoned in the 1980s for criticizing the military regime of Samuel Doe and then backed Charles Taylor's rebellion before falling out with him and being charged with treason after he became president. She has lived in exile twice. In 1997, she stood against Charles Taylor in elections. She has also held important financial positions, from minister of finance in the late 1970s to Africa director at the United Nations Development Programme.

Her first years in office have seen many changes in her country. She has dealt with corruption by sacking officials and demanding transparency in contracts. She has appointed experienced women to run the top ministries – Finance, Justice and Commerce. She is attempting to break down the tribal nature of Liberia's politics and foster a free press and has made education free and compulsory for all primary school children.

In a speech in October 2007 she said: 'It is my hope that when history passes judgment on me, it will not just remark that I was the first woman to be elected President in Africa. I would like to be remembered for raising the bar for accountable governance in Liberia and across the continent; for designing institutions that serve the public interest; for turning a failed state into a thriving democracy with a vibrant, diversified private-sector-driven economy; for sending children back to school; for returning basic services to the cities and bringing them to rural areas. I want Liberia to show the world that in the time of great uncertainty, with sustained support from the United States of America and its partners, a post-conflict country can live in peace within its own borders and amongst its neighbors and emerge as a nation that embraces constitutionally defined separation of powers, that respects civil rights, and the rule of law.'

www.liberiaitech.com/theperspective/2007 and
http://news.bbc.co.uk/1/hi/world/africa

countries in the South. Rwanda has the highest number of women parliamentarians in the world with women constituting nearly 50 per cent in the Chamber of Deputies and about 35 per cent in the Senate.

But it is important to remember just how recent these changes have been. In Switzerland, women only got the vote in 1971 – 123 years after men. In Kuwait, women were only allowed to vote at national level in 2006. In South Africa, white women were allowed to vote in 1931, Indian and 'colored' women in 1984 and black women in 1994.[2] So perhaps it is not so surprising that only 19 countries have achieved the benchmark of 30 per cent representation set in 1995 in the Platform for Action from the UN Women's conference in Beijing. This number actually fell from 20 in 2006.[3] In all these countries, there were legal or voluntary quotas – something that seems to be the key, at least initially, to increasing women's share of seats.

But trumpeting the many achievements cannot hide the fact that in 2007 women still only accounted for an average of 17.2 per cent of parliamentary seats, although this was up from 16.4 per cent in 2006. The overall increase in numbers since 1995 has been 0.5 per cent per year. There is some good news however: a recent survey by the 50/50 Campaign, which was set up in 2000 by the Women's Environment and Development Organization to lobby for equal repre-sentation for women and men in parliaments around the world, found that 'the number of women cabinet ministers is increasing slowly, but steadily. In 1999, women comprised 8.7 per cent of cabinet ministers worldwide. By July 2007 women's representation in national cabinets had risen to 15.2 per cent.' Most of these are in socio-cultural positions.[4]

Professional women

Women are also under-represented at senior levels in all professions – from the UN to trade unions and business. According to recent research conducted by the International Labour Organization (ILO), women make up only 33 per cent of managerial and admin-istrative posts in the developed world; 15 per cent in Africa and 13 per cent in Asia and the Pacific. Women constitute only 14.6 per cent of board directors. According to Rachel Mayanja, Special Adviser of the Secretary-General on Gender Issues and advancement of Women: 'At this rate it will take more than 70 years for women to achieve parity.'[5]

Table 9 – Parliamentary women

The range of representation is enormous; from 0 per cent in 9 countries to nearly half in Rwanda – showing that it is not always the richest countries that rank the highest.

Women's share of seats in national parliaments in selected countries, November 2007

Top 10

Country	Percentage of women in parliament
1 Rwanda	48.8
2 Sweden	47.3
3 Finland	42.0
4 Costa Rica	38.6
5 Denmark	38.0
6 Norway	37.9
7 Netherlands	36.5
8 Cuba	36.0
9 Spain	36.0
10 Mozambique	34.8

Bottom 10

23 countries have women holding fewer than 5% of seats in parliament.

Country	Percentage of women in parliament
128 Papua New Guinea	0.9
129 Yemen	0.3
130 Kyrgyzstan	0.0
131 Micronesia (Fed. States of)	0.0
132 Oman	0.0
134 Palau	0.0
135 Qatar	0.0
136 Saudi Arabia	0.0
137 Solomon Islands	0.0

Inter-Parliamentary Union, January 2008 www.ipu.org/wmn-e/classif.htm

One of the difficulties for a woman of taking on such public positions is that very often the long hours involved take them away from home and family, and there may be no-one at home to do the work. Some women who have reached the top have decided that it is not worth it: Only 10 women are Chief Executive Officers of *Fortune* magazine's 500 largest

Women win the vote in Kuwait

June 2006 was an historic month in Kuwait. Women were allowed to stand and vote in national elections for the first time ever.

Ironically, this was partly due to the fact that the country has the oldest parliamentary tradition in the Gulf, dating back to the early 1960s. This means that each time the idea of votes for women came up in parliament, MPs were able to vote against. In other countries in the region, it is the ruling families who have made the decision.

In 1999, the then Emir Sheikh Jaber al-Ahmad al-Sabah saw his royal decree in favor of women voting rejected by the National Assembly. But finally a bill calling for universal suffrage was passed in parliament in 2005 by 37 MPs, with 21 voting against and one abstaining. Women in the public gallery burst into loud applause when they heard the result.

It was the end of a 40-year battle, and came after continuous blocking by hard-line conservatives and pressure from the royal family. The 1962 election law limits voting to Kuwaiti male citizens, apart from police and the military, over the age of 21. These comprise only 15 per cent of the population. Any woman politician or voter still has to abide by Islamic law. In the 2006 elections, where women ran for parliament seats for the first time, all 30 female candidates (out of a total of 250) were defeated.

In January 2008, there was a march on parliament for women's rights. The only woman in the cabinet, Education Minister Nouriya Al-Sabeeh, had just won a vote of no confidence. 'We're so happy we can fly,' said a woman school principal. 'This is a victory for Kuwaiti women. Let the other half of society work and watch the results,' she added.

www.asianews.it/; other information from http://news.bbc.co.uk/1/hi/world/middle_east

US companies. Of the 108 women who have appeared on this list over the past five years, at least 20 have left their prestigious positions – most of their own volition, like former Pepsi-Cola North America CEO Brenda Barnes (who moved home to Illinois to focus on her family) and former Fidelity Personal Investments president Gail McGovern (now a marketing professor at Harvard Business School).

This is not just true for powerful women in the US. At grassroots level in Cambodia, Pum Hoeun (see box p. 69) has benefited from training with the Female Councillor Forums, which address many of the issues which prevent women seeking political office – low confidence; lack of experience in office; discrimination

Redefining power

Ann Fudge is a Harvard Business School alumni, General Electric board member, wife, mother, grandmother, globetrotter, public service advocate, former star executive at Kraft Foods, and – following a two-year sabbatical during which some surmised that she had killed her career – chairman and CEO of ad conglomerate Young & Rubicam. Inside her makeshift office, currently under renovation, on the 12th floor of Y&R's Madison Avenue headquarters, Fudge announces a mission: 'We need to redefine power!' She's not so naive as to believe that her new clout as an imagemaker equips her to recast such a mystifying thing as power. But there's no harm in trying. Fudge wants to ditch the conventional definition of the term. 'Do we have to follow the boys' scorecard?' she asks.

Source: www.fortune.com/fortune/

Pum Hoeun

Pum Hoeun is second deputy of Angcheum commune, Tbaung Khmom district, Kampong Cham province, Cambodia. Fifty-one-year-old Pum Hoeun, a midwife married with two children, was elected in the 2002 elections. Pum Hoeun represents the opposition party, as a result of which she faced considerable hostility from the commune chief, and from some other male commune council members when she was first elected. By attending the forum, Pum Hoeun learned a great deal about how to deal with others, how to communicate effectively, and how to challenge and overcome discrimination. Her hard work, increased confidence, and improved communication skills have led to her being appointed to lead committees on land dispute, domestic violence, women and children's affairs, and commune development planning. She has also established good relations with the police, and says that she can now go to them at any time and ask them to accompany her to help resolve disputes. Pum Hoeun also secured funding for the commune from various NGOs and donors, for projects to build a bridge in the commune, and to provide toilets for individual houses, directly benefiting disadvantaged members of her constituency.

Pum Hoeun is very proud that she has proved herself to be capable; more importantly, she feels a close affinity to all the members of her commune council as well as the people who elected her. As a result of her efforts to serve her community, Pum Hoeun is now respected and valued by her constituents and the political party she represents. Thanks to this, in 2007 she was re-elected to the post of second deputy in her constituency.

Programme Insights: *Strengthening the Voices of Women Leaders*, Lessons from Cambodia, Oxfam GB 2007.

Empty words or real commitment?

2003 A new Protocol on Women's rights is added to the African Charter on Human and People's Rights. This is the first legal instrument on the rights of African women.

2003 A new Protocol to Prevent, Suppress and Punish Trafficking in Persons, Especially Women and Children was agreed, supplementing the United Nations Convention against Transnational Organized Crime

2001 The World Conference on Racism promised to 'incorporate a gender perspective in all programs of action against racism, racial discrimination, xenophobia and related intolerance'.

2001 The UN AIDS conference, whose motto was: 'Healthy women, healthy world', promised to: 'give priority to the health of women, and, above all, to make sure they have the freedom, the power, and the knowledge to take decisions affecting their own lives and those of their families.'

2000 Optional Protocol to the Women's Convention – for the first time, this allows any woman whose human rights have been violated under the Convention to take her complaint to the UN.

2000 The UN Millennium Declaration committed its signatories to the goal of: 'gender equality and empowerment of women,' saying that achievement of this was critical to the achievement of all the other goals (see box p. 73).

2000 Security Council Resolution 1325 was passed unanimously on 31 October 2000. It is the first resolution ever passed by the Security Council that specifically addresses the impact of war on women, and women's contributions to conflict resolution and sustainable peace.

1996 The World Food Summit acknowledged 'the fundamental contribution to food security by women, particularly in rural areas of developing countries, and the need to ensure equality between men and women.'

1996 The World Conference on Human Settlements (Habitat II) made a commitment to 'enhancing the role of women'.

1995 The Fourth UN World Conference on Women, Beijing – the Beijing Platform for Action mentions 'rights' approximately 500 times and calls for protection of a wide range of women's rights. It is an important document used by women's groups and governments to work on gender equality.

1995 The World Summit on Social Development, Copenhagen – women's organizations persuaded governments to look at the negative impacts on women of macro-economic policies, especially structural adjustment.

1994 The International Conference on Population and Development, Cairo, after much debate, introduced a 20-year policy agenda that is shaping reproductive and sexual health programs and policies around the world. Women's groups succeeded in moving the focus from the reduction of population growth to women's sexual and reproductive health and rights.

1993 The World Conference on Human Rights, in Vienna, stated clearly for the first time that: 'The human rights of women and of the girl-child are an inalienable, integral and indivisible part of universal human rights. The full and equal participation of women in political, civil, economic, social and cultural life, at the national, regional and international levels, and the eradication of all forms of discrimination on grounds of sex are priority objectives of the international community.'

1993 The Declaration on the Elimination of violence against women defines such violence as: 'any act of gender-based violence that results in, or is likely to result in physical, sexual or psychological harm or suffering to women including threats of such acts, coercion or arbitrary deprivation of liberty, whether occurring in public or in private.'

1991 The Rio Declaration on Environment and Development states: 'Women have a vital role in environmental management and development. Their full participation is therefore essential to achieve sustainable development.' Initial drafts had only two references to women; a lobby from women's groups and others ensured that the final document had 170 and a chapter on women's role in the environment.

1990 The World Conference on Education committed itself to 'Education for All' and set targets for gender equality in education.

1979 The International Convention on the Elimination of All Forms of Discrimination against Women (CEDAW) was agreed. This is also known as the Women's Convention and is, essentially, an international bill of rights for women.

from male colleagues; lack of family support; and low visibility as elected officials.

Legal rights

Leadership gives women the possibility of making changes in the laws so that they favor women's rights – although again, there are fewer women than men at the top of the legal profession. Such laws cannot change things overnight, but, as feminist lawyers note, they are a starting point which women can use to their advantage. 'Changes in laws, civil codes, systems of property rights, control over our bodies, labor codes and the social and legal institutions that underwrite male control and privilege are essential if [we] women are to attain justice in society.'[6]

The last 15 years have seen many international legal instruments enacted that apply directly to women, and many more that are not ostensibly about women but which have a number of relevant clauses. Each has built on the previous one – the World Food Summit, for example, reaffirmed its commitment to the Beijing Plan of Action. And they have led to a string of international targets on gender equality – though there have been fewer in recent years.

All treaties have independent supervisory bodies that monitor implementation, encourage compliance and offer guidance. The documents – such as a Plan or Program of Action – which emerge from each conference help to develop new international standards, assist in the implementation of human-rights law at national levels and set benchmarks for policy makers. Though not legally binding upon states, the action programs of key conferences in the 1990s have provided a useful and practical tool to develop policy. This is particularly true of what is now known as CEDAW, or the Women's Convention.

However, the current backlash against women's rights has made women's groups cautious of further conferences and commitments. A statement from the women's organization DAWN (Development Alternatives for a New Era) in April 2003 explains why:

'Contrary to the relatively open environment for such advances that existed during the 1990s, the first decade of the 21st century confronts us with the extreme social conservatism, aggressive unilateralism, and support for militarism of the Bush Administration, and the worsening of fundamentalist trends else-where as well. In such a context, it is very important to protect the gains made for women's human rights through careful and considered action. We believe, in this context, it is imperative that there NOT be any international or regional inter-governmental mee-

Table 10 – More power for women

Lists of targets and international declarations may not seem very exciting, but they mark important milestones that women nationally can use to argue for women's rights.

Targets for women's empowerment at international women's conferences

By the year 2015...	Cairo	Copenhagen	Beijing	Millennium Summit
Provide universal primary education in all countries	•	•	•	•
Reproductive healthcare accessible to all through primary healthcare systems	•	•	•	
Gender equality in education	•			•
Reduce maternal mortality rates by a further 50 %	•		(by 75% since 1990)	•
Life expectancy greater than 70 in countries with highest mortality rates	•			
Eradicate extreme poverty and hunger	•		halve proportion living on $1 a day	•
Increase the proportion of seats held by women in national parliaments			•	• (30%)
Increase the share of women in waged employment in the agricultural sector				
Reduce the spread of HIV/AIDS among 15-24 year old women				•

• is when the targets were set

The Women's Convention

The International Convention on the Elimination of All Forms of Discrimination against Women (CEDAW) requires states to eliminate 'discrimination against women in the enjoyment of all civil, political, economic and cultural rights'. It also establishes programmatic measures for states to pursue in achieving equality between women and men.

Currently, 170 countries – more than two-thirds of the members of the United Nations – have ratified the Convention, committing themselves to a legally binding international treaty, including participation in a country-by-country reporting process. An additional 97 countries have signed the treaty, binding themselves to do nothing in contravention of its terms.

However, it has been a Convention with few teeth. Enforcement has been difficult, and although it represents a strong statement about women's human rights, in practice it is weak and often ignored. Signatories to the Women's Convention have made more reservations to its provisions than any other UN convention.

This was why, after four years of negotiations, the 43rd session of the Commission on the Status of Women adopted an agreed version of the Optional Protocol to CEDAW in March 1999. The negotiation of the Protocol had been controversial and the final version was ultimately a compromise between the strong views of negotiating Nation States. It came into force in December 2000 by which time 13 states had ratified it and 62 had signed it. Amnesty International hailed the Optional Protocol as 'a landmark for women's human rights'.

It brings CEDAW on an equal footing with other international human rights instruments.

The US, on the other hand, is among the few countries that have not ratified CEDAW. The Bush Administration initially identified CEDAW as a 'Category II Treaty', meaning it was 'generally desirable and should be approved'. But, reportedly in response to howls of protest from Bush's ultra-right-wing supporters, the State Department changed its tune, calling the treaty 'vague'. It also indicated that it wants the Justice Department to review the treaty before the Senate votes on it.

Scripps Howard News Service, 'US retreats on UN pact backing women's rights', Lisa Hoffman, 22 July 2002.

tings that in any way involve or may lead to official negotiations.'[7]

The law and the courts

At a regional level, there have been meetings to follow up the women's rights aspects of the Women's Convention in all areas and on all continents. Many of these have been organized by women's groups who have also carried out their own research to find out what impact international action plans have had.

At national level, women have used international laws, in particular the Women's Convention, to lobby their governments to change national laws. One effective way of doing this is to press for the inclusion of women's human rights in national constitutions. In this way, they become the baseline for governmental obligations.

The way in which this happens varies from country to country; some make ratified treaties part of national law. Others include explicit guarantees of gender equality. For example, while the 1986 African Charter on Human and People's Rights does not specifically apply to women, national courts in Botswana, Tanzania and Zimbabwe are using it to make their governments change laws that are discriminatory against women.

In Colombia, organizations including 'feminists and women's organizations' were invited to put proposals for the reform of the constitution. They decided to come together in a single umbrella group which soon grew to include more than 70 NGOs from across the country. It called itself the Women and Constitution Network and today the Colombian constitution contains some of the most 'detailed and substantive guarantees of women's human rights in the world.'[8]

These are not just 'paper equality' but oblige the Government to actively promote the conditions needed to make it real and effective, and to adopt affirmative action if necessary. There is also an enforcement mechanism that individual women can use, via a Constitutional Court.

In South Africa, after the end of apartheid, a coalition of women's NGOs, academics, women politicians, and women's trade union groups presented a charter of women's rights, as a result of which the South African constitution contains a number of

---

Sexual harassment in India

In India, in 1992, a group of women's NGOs brought a petition to the Supreme Court of India. Their petition was motivated by the gang rape of a social worker by her own colleagues in a village in Rajasthan, and the failure of local officials to investigate. However, the problem the NGOs asked the court to address was much broader: there were no laws in India that prohibited sexual harassment in the workplace. Relying on provisions of the Indian constitution, on the Women's Convention and its committee's General Recommendation 19 on violence against women, the NGOs argued that the court should draft a law to compensate for the Indian parliament's inaction.

The legal question the court had to resolve was whether the State actually had an obligation to protect women from sexual harassment. The constitution prohibited discrimination on the basis of sex, and guaranteed just and humane conditions of work, but it didn't refer explicitly to sexual harassment. The court decided in August 1997 that by ratifying CEDAW and by making official commitments at the 1995 Beijing world conference on women, India had endorsed the international standard of women's human rights. According to this standard, gender equality requires protection from sexual harassment.

The court drew up a set of national guidelines, including detailed requirements for processing sexual harassment complaints, which will bind private and public employers until the Government passes suitable legislation. They include a definition of sexual harassment:

'...sexual harassment includes such unwelcome sexually determined behavior (whether directly or by implication) as: a) physical contact and advances; b) a demand or request for sexual favors; c) sexually colored remarks; d) showing pornography; e) any other unwelcome physical, verbal or non-verbal conduct of sexual nature.'

---

significant provisions guaranteeing women's equality. 'Non-sexism' is listed with 'non-racism' as one of the State's fundamental values.

In Africa, common and customary law has generally discriminated against women. For example, in some countries women are not allowed to inherit, own or sell land, or to pass their nationality on to their children. Courts in countries such as Tanzania are beginning to address this problem – nationality laws have been reformed in Mauritius and Zimbabwe and also in other non-African countries including Costa Rica, Italy, Jamaica, Lebanon and Portugal.

The Colombian Constitutional Court

In Colombia, the Constitutional Court has made a number of important decisions involving women's human rights. It has recognized the principle that women's domestic work has real economic value. When called upon to determine a woman's property rights after the death of her common-law husband, the court recognized her domestic work as having contributed to the acquisition and improvement of their home. In another decision, it ordered a high school to re-admit a girl who had been expelled for becoming pregnant. In 1993, the court released a decision regarding the treatment of women prisoners that relied explicitly on the Women's Convention. A challenge was brought over prison regulations that required women prisoners to be fitted with an IUD or take contraceptives prior to conjugal visits but did not make men wear condoms on similar visits. The court ordered that the prison system cease enforcing this regulation, as it violated the constitution's protection against sex discrimination, its guarantee of reproductive and family rights, and the obligation placed on the State to provide women special assistance and protection around pregnancy and birth. The court also found that the regulation was in violation of the Women's Convention.

At the grassroots

Many of these changes in the law, based on international legislation, have come about through pressure from women's non-governmental organizations. But at the grassroots, many women have no idea about laws national or international and no knowledge of how to use them.

A number of organizations are working to change this. Some, like the Association of Black Women Lawyers of New Jersey, were set up to ensure that there were increasing numbers of female lawyers who could improve the quality of legal service. Others, like Women and Law in Southern Africa and Women and Law and Development in Africa, lobby their governments to ratify international human-rights conventions in order to incorporate them into the laws of the land. Some, like SEDEPAC, in Mexico, help poor women to understand and use the law.

Women need both the theory and the practical tools to be able to use legislation to their advantage. They also need the means to get laws changed in favor of women, and this is much easier if women are educated – the subject of the next chapter.

Women in Mexico and the law

Many Mexican women know little about the law. This was the conclusion of research undertaken by SEDEPAC (*Sevicio, Desarollo y Paz, AC*), an organization founded in 1983 to support the activities and education of groups searching for solutions to poverty and marginalization. They established that, in Mexico:

- The majority of women living in poor neighborhoods have no knowledge of existing laws, and even less of their own rights. They feel totally powerless to defend themselves at home or in a legal court. They do not have in their hands the instruments to search for solutions.
- There is an appalling lack of alternative legal services for women in Mexico.
- The existing laws have to be changed, reformed and/or enforced; in order to do this, women must be informed of the law in its existing form, if they are to push for changes.
- The legal system is authoritarian and conservative; therefore it helps to maintain cultural and social stereotypes.

In order to counter these problems, they organized a series of workshops. Margarita Fernanadez, a 24-year-old beautician who did not finish secondary school, was one of those who attended. She works in a grassroots organization with young people in her spare time.

'When the invitation for the workshop arrived, I thought "this is important" because since I started participating in the popular urban struggle I have seen a lot of conflicts and personal problems, affecting both men and women.

'Let me give you some examples: police violence in our poor neighborhoods, the frequency of rapes in our streets, men constantly beating their wives, before the workshop, I could do nothing [about these things]... at the workshop we studied the Penal and Civil codes [and] the Constitution. We have... the legal jargon we need to talk to the judges when we are defending a teenager... Just recently we went to Toluca, [near Mexico City] to defend a *companera* who had been raped, and what we had learned worked! The workshop helped because it gave us theory as well as practical tools.'

Women and Rights, edited by Caroline Sweetman, Oxfam UK and Ireland, 1998.

1 Interviewed for TVE City Life program. **2** *The Atlas of Women*, Joni Seager, Earthscan 2005.**3** Statement by Ms Rachel Mayanja, Special Adviser of the Secretary-General on Gender Issues and Advancement of Women at the 10th session of the Regional Conference on Women in Latin America and the Caribbean, Quito, Ecuador, 6 August 2007 www.un.org/womenwatch/osagi/statements/Quito **4** http://www.wedo.org/files/women **5** ibid **6** DAWN 1987, 81, quoted on p 2 of *Women and Rights*, edited by Caroline Sweetman, Oxfam 1995 **7** www.dawn.org **8** www.UNIFEM.org

6 Education – a matter of life and death

'Going to school has changed my life. I've learnt many things and made friends. I've seen what happens to other kids in my neighborhood who don't go to school. They spend their days sniffing glue, begging for money and getting into trouble. I feel very sorry for them.'
YULENI, 13, VENEZUELA.[1]

Women's and girls' education does not just help the woman concerned; it is key to a country's economic development. But women still make up two-thirds of the world's illiterate people. There is progress, but in many countries it is still slow.

IF THERE IS one single thing that would improve the quality of women's lives – and enable them not only to become lawyers, politicians and businesswomen but simply to take control of their lives – it is education. While this book shows that there are many other areas of women's lives that need improving, education can make a huge difference to them all. 'Enabling girls to attend school is literally a matter of life and death. Education, especially for girls and women, is the best way to break the cycle of ill health, hunger and poverty,' says Kailash Satyarthi, Chairperson of the Global Campaign for Education.[2]

Educating women has huge benefits for the whole community as well as for women themselves:

- It has been shown to increase women's productivity, raising output and reducing poverty.
- It promotes gender equality within households, improves women's ability to make decisions, reduces the number of babies they have and improves maternal health.
- It supports greater participation of girls and women in leadership and decision-making roles.

- Educated women do a better job caring for children, increasing children's chances of surviving to become healthier and better educated.
- It has lasting benefits to future generations and for society as a whole.[3]

There is much to celebrate as we move towards the end of the first decade of the 21st century. By 2005, 63 per cent of countries had equal numbers of boys and girls in primary school and 37 per cent at secondary. UNESCO's 2008 Global Monitoring Report shows that between 1999 and 2005, primary school enrolment increased by 36 per cent in sub-Saharan Africa and 22 per cent in South and West Asia. Worldwide, the number of out-of-school children dropped from 96 million in 1999 to 72 million in 2005.[4]

Among out-of-school children, the proportion of

Table 11 – Schoolgirls

By 2005, 63 per cent of countries had equal numbers of boys and girls in primary school.

Primary school net enrolment/attendance ratio of boys and girls, by region (2000-2006)

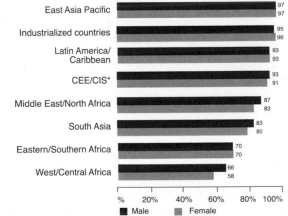

*CEE/CIS – Central and Eastern Europe/Commonwealth of Independent States

Education

http://mdgs.un.org/unsd/mdg/Host.aspx?Content=Data/Trends.htm

Table 12 – Reading and writing

The numbers of literate young women are increasing.

Percentage of the population aged 15-24 years who can both read and write (1995-2004)

	Total	Men	Women
World	**87.4**	**90.3**	**84.4**
Developing Regions	85.0	88.5	81.4
Northern Africa	84.3	89.9	78.4
Sub-Saharan Africa	67.8	72.2	63.8
Latin America and the Caribbean	96.0	95.6	96.5
Eastern Asia	98.9	99.2	98.5
Southern Asia	74.6	82.1	66.6
South-Eastern Asia	96.2	96.4	96.0
Western Asia	91.8	95.5	88.0
Oceania	72.8	74.9	70.5

girls fell from 59 per cent to 57 per cent between 1999 and 2005, although this varied from region to region – in 2005 in sub-Saharan Africa girls accounted for only 54 per cent of out-of-school children, compared with South and West Asia at 66 per cent, and the Arab States at 60 per cent.

The numbers of literate young women are increasing. In 1990, 80.1 per cent of women aged between 15 and 24 were literate as opposed to 88.2 per cent of men, and between 2000 and 2004 it had risen to 84.0 per cent of women and 90.4 per cent of men.[5]

In some countries, especially in Latin America and the Caribbean, and in North America and Western Europe, girls outnumber boys in secondary education. In Latin America and the Caribbean, it is boys, particularly from poor families, who are more likely to drop out of school. A study conducted in Chile found that poor boys are four times more likely to enter the workforce than poor girls. In Brazil, child labor has robbed boys of an education by luring them away from books with promises of money.

The news for girls is not all good. Two-thirds of illiterate people are women. Women and out-of-school girls are by far the largest group without access to

Clarissa's story

Clarissa was only six when she insisted that she wanted to go to school. Her mother Assinou, a small trader in Benin, tried to dissuade her, saying that she could not afford to educate Clarissa. 'You are a girl, you must remain at home. Only boys go to school,' she said. None of Clarissa's three elder sisters went to school. But eventually her mother agreed.

Clarissa's classroom, built of bamboo, has 50 pupils of whom only 15 are girls. In other words, the situation of girls has room for improvement in this village and Jeannette Ahokpè, the supervisor of the education programme of UNICEF has her work cut out for her. Jeannette covers by motorcycle the 10 villages of Zakpota and visits parents to persuade them to enroll their daughters in school.

Clarissa's mother is today the secretary of a group of women who specialize in the manufacture of cassava flour under a UNICEF micro-credit program. 'The profits that we make,' she said, 'will enable us to send our children, particularly our daughters, to school. We no longer have the right to keep them at home.'

'I want to study so that I no longer have to live in poverty,' said Clarissa. 'If I study hard, I will get a good job and be able to help my mother. That is what the teacher told me.' She lives this poverty every day at the school in this arid and impoverished village. 'Our life is very difficult,' explained little Clarissa. 'At recreation time, I have only 25 CFA francs with which to buy my maize porridge. I am sometimes sad.' Her mother hopes that her daughter will not have as hard a life as hers.

Clarissa's mother, who at 35 years old seems 20 years older, worn out by a life of hard work and privations, has a tender look and attitude towards her daughter. 'I will fight until my last breath to ensure that my daughter does not have the same life as I have had. She must study hard in order to be happy, not like me.'

www.ungei.org/reallives/benin_678.html

education. Projections show that on current trends the Millennium Development Goal of eliminating gender disparities at both primary and secondary levels will be missed in 2015 in over 90 countries. Nearly one in five people – 774 million in total – do not have basic literacy skills. More than three-quarters of these live in 15 densely populated countries. Women make up 64 per cent of this number, a share that has changed little in the last 20 years. Disparities between men and women are particularly marked in South and West Asia, the Arab States and sub-Saharan Africa.

Losing out
- Women make up two thirds of illiterates.
- Girls comprise about 57 per cent of all out-of-school children.

Even if they get to school, girls are more likely than boys to drop out after a few years. Once they get to school, the problems do not end. In addition, the quality of the education they receive is often low, with large classrooms and few resources. There are not enough female teachers to give girls support and to act as role models. Lack of education affects a girl's chance of a better life and has a detrimental effect on society as a whole. There is still a long way to go.

Why don't girls go to school?

'If you have a situation where women and girls are discriminated against in society and not all children are in school, it follows almost as night follows day that girls will be kept out of school,' says Christopher Colclough of the Institute of Development Studies (IDS) in Sussex, England, who conducted a 9-country research project in sub-Saharan Africa.[6]

Thus, women's status in society has a direct effect on the number of girls attending school. School is often perceived as a lower priority for girls than for boys, especially when parents have to pay and can only afford to send some of their children. In many countries, the costs of schooling have risen as part of the privatization of education.

'A lot of girls are dropping out of school or not being sent at all because of the poverty of parents,' says Peninah Mlama, executive director of the Forum for African Women Educationalists (FAWE). 'Traditional cultural attitudes are still very strong, especially in rural areas. The little money parents have to scrounge for sending children to school is seen as too big an investment to risk on the girl child.'[7]

Schools may also be far away, making it more of a problem for girls to get to them. Or families prefer to keep girls at home to help with childcare and other chores. In addition, more girls than boys drop out of school. This may be due to discriminatory attitudes, practices and behavior by teachers, parents, and community members and to the fact that there are few female role models. Girls at school may find that the curriculum teaching methodologies and even text books have a gender bias which makes them feel uncomfortable. In all the countries where the IDS team conducted their research, they found that teachers believed boys were more intelligent than girls.

In addition, where girls marry early, they are not expected to go to school, and girls who fall pregnant may be expelled.

Girls in all countries often face sexual harassment – and worse – at school but may be afraid to speak out. Sometimes this is because the teacher is the perpetrator. Lack of action on the part of school authorities, even in the most appalling cases, can lead to girls being afraid to go to school, as this South African 13-year old, who had been raped by her classmates, pointed out: 'After the school break, my mom asked me if I wanted to go back to school. I said no. All the people who I thought were my friends had turned against me. And they [the rapists] were still there. I felt disappointed. [Teachers] always told me they were glad to have students like me, that they wished they had more students like me. If they had made the boys leave, I wouldn't have felt so bad about it.'[8]

What can be done?
If more girls are to be educated, schools need to take steps themselves, and measures must also be taken at government level. Governments are looking at ways of improving gender equality in schools – by increasing the number of women teachers, ensuring that schools

Schools under attack

A 2007 study by UNESCO showed that attacks on schools in countries in conflict are increasing: 'The number of reported targeted attacks on students and educational staff and institutions appears to have risen dramatically in the past three years.' The motives for this are not always to do with opposition to girls' education – though in Afghanistan, for example, this is clearly the case – but have a dramatic impact on schooling. Up to 40 per cent of the 77 million children in the world who are not attending school can be found in conflict or post-conflict countries. Some of the most affected countries are:

Afghanistan: 62 bombing, arson and missile attacks against education targets in 2005 and 88 in 2006, plus 37 threatened attacks.

Colombia: 310 teachers were murdered between 2000 and 2006, and 11,000 children aged 7 to 13 were combatants in 2003.

Iraq: 280 academics have been killed since the fall of Saddam Hussein, 296 education staff were killed in 2005, and 180 teachers were killed between February and November 2006.

Myanmar/Burma: In 2002 an estimated 70,000 child soldiers were enlisted, many of them in the national army, some forcibly recruited as young as 11.

Nepal: Between 2002 and 2006 some 10,600 teachers and 22,000 students were abducted by Maoists, 734 teachers and 1,730 students were arrested or tortured, and 79 schools and one university were destroyed.

Thailand: 71 teachers were killed and 130 schools burned down in 2004-2006.

Shugofa Sahar, a 12-year-old student at the Aysha-e-Durani High School for Girls, said: 'All the girls and boys from Afghanistan should go to school in order to rebuild and develop our country.' But for many children in countries in conflict this is still a distant dream.

'Education under attack, a global study on targeted political and military violence against education staff, students, teachers, union and government officials, and educational institutions', UNESCO, April 2007, http://unesdoc.unesco.org; Integrated Regional Information Networks (IRIN), 14 March 2005; 'New campaign to encourage girls into school', Kabul. www.afghan-web.com/woman/encouragegirlsschool.html'

are close enough for girls to travel safely, and reducing or eliminating school fees for girls. But there are other problems – waiving school fees does not address the question of how to replace a girl's labor at home or in the fields, nor the bias in some countries against educating daughters.

'Nearly every single policy document mentions girls' education, it's almost as if it is the politically correct

'What will it take to get your daughter to school?'

In hundreds of villages in Turkey, in schools and homes and coffee houses, that is the question being asked by teachers, journalists, local activists and religious leaders.

Some 500,000 girls in Turkey do not attend classes. But thanks to a major education drive, approximately 120,000 have enrolled in the last two years.

The campaign, dubbed 'Hey Girls, Let's Go to School,' depends on a vast network of volunteers who go door-to-door to lobby parents on the value of education.

In Van, where the nationwide campaign was launched in 2003, poverty and cultural traditions have historically kept girls at home. Up to half of all girls in this eastern province are estimated to be out of school. Yet through the efforts of the campaign, 20,000 girls have enrolled for the first time. Among its many successes the campaign counts increased media visibility and support from prominent politicians, including the Prime Minister and First Lady of Turkey. Numerous spin-off projects have been created to help raise funds for schools, and a growing number of volunteers are signing up from a wide variety of professions.

Yet persistent poverty and insufficient resources continue to plague the national education system, with dire results for children. Schools are scarce and overcrowded; conditions in urban slums and rural areas are especially bad. And for families that are struggling to afford food for their children, even the most basic school supplies can be well out of reach.

At a community meeting in Van, women respond favorably to a campaign coordinator's speech on the importance of education. But murmurs arise when the volunteer, a respected local high school principal named Bahri Yildizbas, tells them that it is their duty as parents to send their children to school.

'We want education, but we don't have the money,' says one mother. 'The school is far away – it takes too much time to get there, and it's not safe,' says another.

While these practical obstacles hamper progress, the campaign has helped create a hunger for change that promises to pay dividends for decades to come.

According to Zozan Ozgokce, the head of the Van Women's Association and another volunteer who visits local homes, there is a growing consensus that education is an imperative for every child.

'When we ask women how they want their children to live, they almost never say, "like me". And when we ask the women what they want to be, they say, "educated".

'It might take 25 years for the effects of this campaign to show,' she says. 'But the campaign will still be visible then – because it is this generation that will show how the world can be.'

www.ungei.org/gapproject/turkey_422.html

language to use,' says Peninah Mlama. 'But governments don't have the capacity and commitment to really do something.' Mary Joy Pigozzi, a senior UNICEF education adviser, adds: 'If there is one lesson we have learned, it's that there is no single quick fix, but there are usually two or three actions together that are catalytic.'

Two of the most important are involving parents and communities in schools and improving the quality of education. Pigozzi says that this has to happen through affirmative action that acknowledges how different a girl's situation may be from her brother's. 'You have to understand that girls may get less protein than boys, that communities raise girls to have different expectations of themselves. Then you have to look at the quality of the learning environment to address issues such as safety and sexual harassment, and the whole teaching-learning process.'[9]

Literacy

Women's literacy is also vital for any kind of national development. There are a number of programs which promote literacy alongside a range of other measures to help women gain confidence and economic independence. The Dhaka Ahsania Mission is one such organization that has been changing women's lives across Asia.

Six years ago, the NGO started classes in a village in western Bangladesh. It was a big step to take. The women were not allowed out; they could not meet strangers even if they visited their homes, and most had never been to school. 'By tradition we could not even pronounce our husband's name,' said Hira Akhtar. When she asked permission to go to classes from her husband, who could barely pen a signature himself, he threw up his hands. 'What will happen by reading all these books?' he asked. But these were not ordinary books and the classes were not like at a school. The NGO opened membership to representatives of the 250 poorest families out of the 311 families in the village – those earning less than 2,700 taka ($47) a month – and ensured that 75 per cent of them were the most disadvantaged members of those families: women.

The classes concentrate on literacy, numeracy, and subjects relevant to the learners' lives. More than 50,000 of the poorest people will this year be using their self-learning guides to learn how to read and write. A crucial factor in the success of the centers is that each is run by a committee of members and comes together to discuss issues concerning the whole village.

A survey of Rogaghurampur, a 100-household village of 450 people in Jessore district, where 63 families had been active members since 1998, has documented the dramatic changes since the center began its work. By December 2002, the percentage of literate families had more than doubled from 30 to 65 per cent; the number using latrines and fuel-efficient ovens had soared; the practice of marrying children off at 13 or younger had been wiped out with knock-on effects on the number and spacing of pregnancies; the role of women in decision-making and earning an income had been completely transformed and the percentage of girls going to school jumped from 30 to 100 per cent. Today Hira's husband asks her to borrow books for him to read. 'In the early days, many of the women who returned home late from the classes were beaten. Men didn't think we should leave the house for anything,' said Hira. 'But now attitudes have changed completely. The status of women has been raised a lot. Now if someone says your wife needs to go for training in Dhaka, the husband will gladly agree.'

There are many projects like this one, which teach women to read and to help girls to get to school and stay there. But they also need training – vocational, practical and on the job – an area where women and girls often miss out and which affects their ability to improve their work, earn more money and develop their potential.

But as long as poverty and cultural norms that favor boys, exist, and the political will is lacking, it will take a long time for any targets to be reached. And in the meantime, female babies will be born, develop into young women, bear children and die without ever seeing the inside of a schoolroom.

1 UNICEF, *The State of the World's Children 2004*. 2 www.ungei.org/ 3 United Nations Girls' Education Initiative. 4 http://portal.unesco.org 5 http://mdgs.un.org/unsd/mdg/Host.aspx?Content=Data/Trends.htm. 6 *Unesco Courier*, 2001 www.unesco.org/courier/2001_05/uk/education. htm 7 *Unesco Courier*, 2001 www.unesco.org/courier/2001_05/uk/education.htm 8 Human Rights Watch. 2001, *Scared at School: Sexual Violence against Girls in South African Schools*. 9 *Unesco Courier*, 2001 www.unesco. org/courier/2001_05/uk/education.htm10 www.unesco.org/education

7 Canaries of the eco-crisis: women and the environment

'As the majority of the world's poor, women play decisive roles in managing and preserving biodiversity, water, land and other natural resources, yet their centrality is often ignored or exploited.' KLAUS TOEPFER, EXECUTIVE DIRECTOR UNITED NATIONS ENVIRONMENT PROGRAMME[1]

Changes to the environment are gender-specific. Women are rarely able to take part in decisions about the environment, whether the issue is privatization of water, ownership of land or the patenting of seeds. But they have done much to protect it, sometimes at great risk to themselves.

IS THERE A difference between women's relationship to the environment and men's? What does this have to do with women's rights? Does climate change affect women differently from men?

At first glance, the environment of the world we live in, and sustainable ways to develop it, does not seem to be gender-specific. Climate change and global warming, deforestation, pollution, the depletion of global water resources, environmental degradation and disaster affect every human being on the planet, whatever their sex. But in fact, research shows that environmental issues can affect men and women very differently. This can be illustrated by women's relationship to water. While women often have clearly defined responsibilities around drinking, they rarely have control over water resources or access to decision-making about water. And yet, says Indian environmentalist Vandana Shiva: 'In the Third World women carry the water to get it home. They are the first ones to know water is polluted. They are the first to know the well has run dry. They are the first to know water is saline.

They are the canary of the eco-crisis.'[2] They are also often at the forefront of environmental battles.

Privatizing the earth

Privatization, industrial logging, over-fishing, toxic dumping, mining... the effects of the free market and globalization on the environment and the threat that this poses to its sustainability are well-documented. The latest solution to the world's environmental problems, it seems, is not to cut down on our use of fossil fuels, or to find better ways of conserving water and less polluting chemicals for everyday use, but to privatize environmental resources.

The issue of privatization has particular problems for women. For example, in Ghana and elsewhere the privatization of water has led to an increase in water-borne diseases such as typhoid, cholera and guinea-worm among the poor who cannot afford to pay for clean water. A bucket of water costs up to a tenth of people's daily earnings in cities. And finding water for their families has become an even bigger

---

No more plastic bags

Supriya Sahu is not an obvious fighter. But as District Collector in the Ooty region of Southern India, she has taken on the business lobby in her effort to ban plastic bags from the area.

And she has won. A law has been enacted. Large signposts greet visitors entreating them to 'Enjoy your stay in the Nilgiris, but please do not use plastic'. Chellerams, one of the biggest stores, was fined 1,000 rupees for disregarding the ban.

All over the district, the ubiquitous traditional Tamil *manja pye*, a colored cloth bag, has made its reappearance. Meat and fish are wrapped in leaves as they used to be 10 years ago. And school children frequently go on plastic picking treks.

In this ecologically sensitive and tourism-prone region plastics had not only caused mountains of litter but suffocated animals, choked drainage and water supply channels and polluted Ooty Lake.

Young, bright and determined, Supriya Sahu has begun the process of reversing the damage.

www.hinduonnet.com/thehindu/2002/05/26/stories

Brazil's 'widows of drought'

The semi-arid north-eastern portion of Brazil is highly populated, with periodic droughts that spawn encroaching deserts, unequal distribution of land and severe hardships for most people. The migration of men on a large scale leaves women to run their households. They become known as 'widows of drought' as in many cases their husbands never send any promised remittances home and neglect to return.

Leading women activists Rosilda Silva Cruz and Vanete Almeida, members of the largely male Rural Labourers' Union, are now mobilizing women's participation in development activities in the region. They both began their community involvement at an early age and have worked in grass-roots movements since that time.

Ms Silva Cruz, one of only four women in the union's directorate, coordinates six women's action groups and takes an active part in radio broadcasts disseminating information on drought and environmental degradation, and also on political issues affecting rural women workers. Ms Almeida helped to organize the first Rural Women Workers' Meeting in the region, and has since branched out to make international connections with women leaders combating desertification. 'We believe in what we are doing,' she says with pride.

www.undp.org/seed/unso/women/film.htm; Branco, 1999, quoted in 'Women and the Environment, United Nations Environment Programme', www.unep.org/PDF/Women/ChapterFour.pdf

burden for women. Says Hawa Amadu, who lives in one of Accra's slum areas: 'Sometimes I go without food so my grandchildren will have water... Soon we will have to drink air.'[3]

Privatization of land, however, can have positive effects if women are allowed to own and control it. Florence Nnali, a landless farmworker in Uganda who survives by collecting wild cassava for herself and her six children, says: 'Land in Uganda is wealth. You cannot have land and starve. If you have land you can plant crops on it, sell it and be buried on it.'[4]

But there is a hidden danger, says environmentalist Bina Agarwal. The buying of land by women can be 'used by pro-liberalization lobbies to open up indigenous systems of land tenure to market forces and foreign commercial interests.'[5]

> ## Green beans
> When Irene Kathambi's husband first sold her the idea of growing French beans in Marathi village, Meru, in Kenya, she thought she would have equal claim over the proceeds. 'I do most of the work on the farm such as digging, planting, weeding and picking. But my husband receives the payments and gives me what he pleases after we have sold the crop,' she says.
>
> There are many women like Irene Kathambi, whose husbands have either compelled them to grow green beans on their plots, or retracted their right to these plots entirely. A study notes that 'export horticulture' has changed from being a predominantly female sphere to a mixed on, which has a knock on effect on property control. It estimates that women carry out more than 70 per cent of the labor for French beans but receive only 30 per cent of the income. Under the traditional system of land rights in Kenya, women have the right to cultivate usufruct land but not to own it – and access is usually given through a male relative.
>
> Like Irene, most Meru women don't inherit or own land. Armed with only 'use rights', women cannot prevent men from encroaching on their plots.
>
> Francis Ayieko in *Food for All? Can hunger be halved?* John Madeley, Panos Institute, 2001.

Women's health

The environment has an effect on women's health as well as their income. Millions of women forced to cook on open fires, for example, or to carry heavy containers long distances every day to collect water, may find that their health suffers as a result. Pollution and pesticide use also cause problems for women; there is a link between environmental pollution and cancers such as breast cancer. And endocrine-disrupting chemicals have been shown to breach the placenta, reach babies in the womb, and infect breast milk, resulting in thyroid problems, delayed sexual development and sometimes lower IQ in children.[6] Other chemicals can cross national boundaries, and build up in the food chain. These are known as POPs – Persistent Organic Pollutants. Nine of the 12 most polluting and harmful to health are pesticides, used extensively in agriculture. And 60 to 70 per cent of the world's farmers and agricultural workers are women – 80 per cent in some parts of Africa. The World Health Organization estimates that at least three million people are poisoned by pesticides every year and more than 200,000 die.[7]

In Malaysia, for example, many women work on the plantations and spray pesticides. They suffer from sore eyes, skin complaints, burnt fingernails and disrupted menstruation. Pregnant women have been known to lose their babies or give birth to deformed babies. Veena is one of the sprayers: 'I have been spraying pesticides for the past 20 years. I spray paraquat[8] all the time. It is so strong that the odor makes me sick most of the time. In the beginning I used to cry. Now my only main problem is nose bleed and chest pain. I also have bad stomach pain.'[9]

Climate change and disasters

Climate change and disasters also have a direct impact on poor women, who are responsible for family and community care, and as such are key to the survival of both. Environmental crises mean that they have to spend even more time finding food and shelter, and walking further to fetch water or cut firewood. 'Growing desertification caused by changed farming practices in fragile ecosystems also forces women to walk for miles in search of water,' says Madhukar Upadhya, research director of the Nepal Water Conservation Foundation. 'Women in Sindh in Pakistan walk up to 10 miles to fetch water and women with pitchers trudging up steep slopes is a common sight in the hills.'[10]

And yet neither the Kyoto Protocol nor the UN Framework Convention for Climate Change (UNFCCC) make any mention of gender, and there has been very little research or discussion on the effects of climate change on women.

In 1998 Hurricane Mitch affected more than two million people in Honduras and Nicaragua alone.

Damages were estimated at $5 billion. Small producers, street children and female-headed households were hardest hit. Women had to maintain their households, help organize the community and find work in the informal economy. They had more to do, and less to eat. After the disaster, men had generally tried to go back to their old jobs, but women found it more difficult because of their many responsibilities. Cultural roles may make women more at risk than men during environmental disasters. Disasters aside, even a heavy rainy season or a drought can have a significant impact on the hours women have to put in just to keep themselves and their families alive.[11] 'The disproportionate share of the burden of poverty borne by women has a two-fold impact,' says Madhukar Upadhya. 'On the one hand, their workload for family survival increases and on the other, their share in food and nutrition intake decreases further. In almost all countries of the region [South Asia] women do not have an adequate calorific intake in their diet and many pregnant women suffer from anemia.'[12]

Indigenous women in particular, who have a close relationship with the land on which they live, are deeply affected by changes to their environment: 'Our entire life depends on forests. We get firewood from forests, wood for house construction and also fodder for our cattle... We also get grass, leaves, precious herbs and minerals for our animals. In addition, forests give us tea leaves, humus, fertilizer,' says Lakupati, an 80-year-old tribal woman from Kinnaur, India.[13]

However, there is a growing realization that climate change affects women differently from men. In 2003 at the 9th Conference of the Parties to the United Nations Framework Convention on Climate Change, a network of people interested in gender issues was established. The network organized workshops on gender and climate at both the Tenth and Eleventh Confer-ences. Since the tsunami in late 2004, development projects are also looking at the different situations of men and women. As one article notes: 'It would seem that this issue is about to be discovered.'[14]

A study in Germany found a number of differences between women and men in their attitudes to climate change:

- Women and men perceive and assess risks differently, and that is also true for climatic change. More than 50 per cent of the women, but only 41 per cent of the men, classify climate change caused by global warming as extremely or very dangerous.
- Trust placed in the role played by environmental policy also varies according to gender. More women than men are skeptical that Germany can cope with problems resulting from climate change. Nonetheless, some 62.9 per cent of the women, but only 53.8 per cent of the men, are in favor of a pioneering role for Germany in climate policy.
- Women are more willing to alter environmentally harmful behavior. They do not rely as much on science and technology to solve environmental problems to the exclusion of lifestyle changes. As a result, they place a higher value on the influence exerted by each and every individual on preventing climate change.
- Studies show that women have a definite information deficit on climate politics and climate protection.
- The instruments used to prevent climate change are probably also gender-biased.[15]

Patenting

Indigenous women have been heavily involved in opposing the patenting of products, plants and processes through what is known as the agreement on Trade Related Aspects of Intellectual Property Rights (TRIPS). This agreement, signed in 1993, extends international patenting rights to all members of the World Trade

---

Women in the tsunami

Even the effects of climate change may affect women differently from men. During the tsunami in Asia, many more women than men died. This was because:

- More men than women could swim.
- Women stayed behind to rescue children and the elderly.
- Women stayed indoors waiting for men to fetch them because they were not supposed to leave home alone.

After the tsunami, the most effective relief efforts relied on and supported women to rebuild their communities.

Organization and stipulates that all member countries must introduce a new and standardized level of patent protection. Diverse Women for Diversity, a women's organization, argues that the patenting of seeds and other natural resources such as the *neem* tree has an adverse effect on rural women: 'Intellectual property rights (IPRs)… will dispossess rural women of their power, control and knowledge. IPRs… aim to take seed out of peasant women's custody and medical plants out of the hands of women healers and make it the private property of transnational companies (TNCs).'[16]

In effect, their argument is that the patenting of seeds not only threatens biodiversity by giving companies 'ownership' of seeds, but undermines women's roles as the guardians and custodians of plants, whether as farmers or as traditional healers. In India, for example, 'there are 7,500 species used as medicinal plants by the indigenous medical traditions of India. These traditions are kept alive by over 400,000 [practitioners], in addition to millions of housewives, birth attendants and herbal healers using village-based health traditions. Seventy per cent of health care needs in India are still based on traditional systems using medicinal plants. Eighty per cent of seeds used by farmers still come from farmers' seed supply. India is thus still a predominantly biodiversity-based economy and women's knowledge is very central to this economy.'

Women fight back

And yet women have been mainly absent from most of the big decisions taken about the environment. At the sixth Conference of Parties to the UNFCC meeting (known as CoP6) in The Hague in November 2000, women's issues were barely on the agenda, although chairperson Jan Pronk when interviewed afterwards noted that: 'In developing countries women are often the primary providers and users of energy. Therefore, the participation of women and women's organizations is crucial.'

The fact that women's issues were not part of the debate was all the more surprising in that as many as 20 per cent of environment ministers at the conference were women and so were representatives from three main non-governmental organizations: Friends of the Earth, Worldwide Fund for Nature and the Climate Action Network.[17] 'Some of the key NGO negotiators are women, who may even be interested in gender issues at an individual level and yet in the heat of the negotiations, they seem to get absorbed by the complex technical issues.' says Gotelind Alber of the Climate Alliance.[18]

In other international fora, women are generally discussed only as an add-on, as Jyothi Parika of the West African NGO ENDA Tiers-Monde noted in her workshop – which was the only one on women – at CoP8 (on climate change) in New Delhi in October 2002. Many women at such conferences – including the World Summit on Social Development in 2002 in Johannesburg – call for capacity building and advocacy work to improve women's voices at these conferences.

Women are also absent from senior levels in businesses dealing with the environment – in the energy sector in Germany, for example, women make up six per cent of technical staff, four per cent of decision-makers and only one per cent of senior managers.''Many countries in the South have a much better track record than in the North in encouraging women to follow technical studies,'[19] notes Ulrike Röhr, a German civil engineer and founder of *Frauen Umweltnetz* (Women's Environmental Network).

Defending the environment

But increasingly, women are joining together to defend their environment and to present sustainable solutions. In the 1970s, the women of the Chipko movement in northern India saved the forests in their area by attaching themselves to individual trees to stop these being cut down. Since then, thousands of women's groups from the grassroots to the international have formed. Some are very specific, like the Chipko, or ENERGIA or AWLAE (African Women Leaders in Agriculture and the Environment). Others work on a range of issues – a few examples from the many are Environment and Development Action in the Third World (ENDA-TM); Women's Environmental Networks in various European countries; Diverse Women for Diversity; the Grassroots Organizations Operating Together in Sisterhood (GROOTS), and the Women's Environment and Development Network (WEDO).

At the 1992 UN Conference on Environment and Development women came up with their own comprehensive blueprint for change. Formulated by 1,500 women from 83 countries and covering a broad range of critical issues, the Women's Action Agenda 21 helped galvanize women worldwide to push for their priorities in international institutions, governments, the private sector and civil society. There are now 3,500 Local Agenda 21s in the world – though only six in the US.

In the lead-up to the 2002 UN World Summit on Sustainable Development (WSSD) in Johannesburg, women around the world collaborated to update and revitalize the agenda for change. The new Women's

Action Agenda for a Peaceful and Healthy Planet 2015 is a vision for the future and a document of principles that people worldwide can contribute to and use for their own advocacy globally, nationally and locally. It covers peace and human rights, globalization for sustainability, access and control of resources, environmental security and health and governance for sustainable development.

Women's rights and environmental improvement go hand-in-hand: 'The sustainable use of natural resources can only be achieved in the long term if the approach includes the concept of women's autonomy. An Action Aid study of girls in Nepal showed how efforts to improve girls' education had been stymied by environmental degradation. Deforestation and erosion led to economic stress within households, and girls were consequently kept out of school to help at home.[20] However, women's autonomy can only be strengthened if account is taken of elements relating to the use of natural resources,' says a paper from the Dutch Ministry of Foreign Affairs.[21] The next section

Global gender and climate change alliance launched

In January 2008, the Global Gender and Climate Change Alliance was launched. Under the auspices of the United Nations Environment Programme, UNDP, the International and the Women's Environment and Development Organization, it will:

- Provide support to UNFCCC and its bodies to ensure that the UN mandates on gender equality are fully implemented.
- Ensure that UN financing mechanisms on mitigation and adaptation address the needs of poor women and men equitably.
- Set standards and criteria for climate change mitigation and adaptation that incorporate gender equality and equity principles.
- Build capacity at global, regional and local level to design and implement gender-responsive climate change policies, strategies and programs.
- Establish a network for learning, knowledge exchange and advocacy on gender and climate change.

www.wedo.org

profiles a woman in the forefront of the fight to pre-serve natural resources.

Wangari Maathai

In 2004, Dr Wangari Muta Maathai became the first African woman to receive the Nobel Peace Prize for 'her contribution to sustainable development, democracy and peace'. She is a Member of Parliament in Kenya and served as Assistant Minister for Environment and Natural Resources between January 2003 and November 2005.

Her environmental activism goes back a long way. In 1964 she founded the National Council of Women in Kenya. In 1977 she started the Greenbelt Movement to counter the environmental consequences of deforestation and desertification and to educate people about development that is truly sustainable. Greenbelt started with a tree nursery in Maathai's garden; today over 30 million trees have been planted in Kenya and there are 5,000 tree nurseries. Projects in other countries have also modeled themselves on Greenbelt.

'The biggest impact,' says Maathai, 'has been the sense of hope and power in the lives of the ordinary women who comprise 90 per cent of the members. They can hardly read or write. Yet they often join the movement not from personal need; instead they need to help their family – they need to get money to pay their children's school fees or to buy their clothes or to build a house. And the women respond so quickly to a common cause that soon they see this as a way to help the community at large – and the nation. They want to make a contribution.'

Maathai was also the former chairperson of the National Council of Women of Kenya. She has been imprisoned several times. In the 1980s her husband Mwangi Mathai, a politician whom she had married in 1969, divorced her, saying she was too strong-minded for a woman and that he was unable to control her. The judge in the divorce case agreed with the husband, and Wangari was put in jail for speaking out against the judge, who then decreed that she must drop her husband's surname. In defiance, Wangari chose to add an extra 'a' instead. In 1989 she saved Nairobi's Uhuru Park by stopping the construction by then President Moi's business associates of the 60-story Kenya Times Media Trust business complex.

She has run for the presidency a number of times. In 2003 she founded the Mazingira Green Party of Kenya. In March 2005 she was elected president of the African Union's Economic, Social and Cultural Council. She was defeated in parliamentary elections of December 2007 and called for a recount in her constituency, saying that both sides should feel the outcome was fair and that there were indications of fraud. In January 2008, as violence erupted in Kenya after the elections, Maathai and the Green Belt Movement set up a peace tent in Nairobi, listening to victims of violence and collecting signatures on a petition demanding dialogue between President Mwai Kibaki and the leader of the opposition, Raila Odinga. Maathai blamed the Government for doing little to prevent the ethnic driven killings in the country and planted a tree as a symbol of renewal and hope.[22]

Violence against women is the subject of the next chapter.

1 www.unep.org/PDF/Women/foreword.pdf 2 www.inmotionmagazine. com/global/vshiva3.html#Anchor-Women-3800 3 'Water: every drop counts', New Internationalist 354, March 2003. 4 'No way out for Uganda's Chronically poor? Sharon Lamwaka, Panos Features, June 2003. 5 B Agarwal, 'The Gender and Environment Debate' in Political Ecology: global and local, ed Keil Roger, Routledge, 1998. 6 Theo Colburn, www.wwf.org 7 'Pick your poison: the pesticide scandal' New Internationalist 323, May 2000. 8 Paraquat is one of the 12 dangerous pesticides listed by the Pesticide Action Network, www.pan-international.org 9 'Victims without voice, a study of women pesticide workers in Malaysia', V Arumugam, Tenaganita and Pesticides Action Network Asia Pacific, www.pan-international.org 10 'Justice for All: promoting environmental justice in South Asia', Panos South Asia, August 2002, www.panos.org.np 11 'Uncertain predictions,

invisible impacts and the need to mainstream gender in climate change adaptations', Valerie Nelson, Kate Meadows, Terry Cannon, John Morton and Adrienne Martin in *Gender Development and Climate Change*, edited by Rachel Masika, Oxfam 2002. **12** Justice for All: promoting environmental justice in South Asia', Panos South Asia, August 2002, www.panos.org.np **13** Quoted in *High Stakes: the future for mountain societies*, Panos, May 2002. **14** 'Gender and climate change' Ulrike Röhr *Tiempo*, issue 59, April 2006, www.tiempocyberclimate.org/portal/archive/pdf/tiempo59high.pdf **15** ibid. **16** www.diversewomen.org/Issues.htm **17** N Wamykonya and M Skutsch 'COP6: The gender issue forgotten?' in ENERGIA News 4 (1) March 2001. **18** ENERGIA News vol 5 no 4, 2002. **19** 'Differences and similarities: a North-South Comparative Analysis' in ENERGIA News Vol 5 no 4, 2002 **20** 'Listening to Smaller Voices: Children in an environment of change', V Johnson, J Hill and E Ivan Smith, Action Aid 1995. **21** 'Gender and Environment: a delicate balance between profit and loss', NEDA, 1997. **22** www.greenbeltmovement.org/a.php?id=280; www.chatham.edu/rci/well/women11-20/maathai.html; http://nobelprize.org/nobel_prizes/peace/laureates/2004/maathai-bio.html

8 A devastating toll: violence against women

'Violence against women and girls continues unabated in every continent, country and culture. It takes a devastating toll on women's lives, on their families, and on society as a whole. Most societies prohibit such violence – yet the reality is that too often, it is covered up or tacitly condoned.' UN SECRETARY-GENERAL BAN KI-MOON, 8 MARCH 2007[1]

The last century was the most violent in history, and much of this was against women, both in war and peace. Little seems to have changed as we near the end of the first decade of the twenty-first. Violence in many forms is used to control women, but men and women have been taking action to reduce it – and sometimes succeeded.

AT LEAST ONE out of every three women around the world has been beaten, coerced into sex, or otherwise abused in her lifetime – with the abuser usually someone known to her.[2] UNIFEM, the United Nations Fund for Women, says violence against women is: 'Perhaps the most pervasive human rights violation that we know today, it devastates lives, fractures communities, and stalls development.'[3] For women aged 15 to 44 years, violence is a major cause of death and disability.[4] Half the women who die from homicides are killed by current or former husbands or partners. Studies have also shown that violence can also be connected to the spread of HIV; for example, a survey among 1,366 South African women showed that women who were beaten by their partners were 48 per cent more likely to be infected with HIV than those who were not.[5] And unlike many other kinds of violence, sexual violence crosses race, class and religious divides. It is as common in the rich world as the poor.

Crossing continents

- More than half the women in Bangladesh, Ethiopia, Peru and Tanzania in a World Health Organization (WHO) study reported physical or sexual violence by intimate partners. In rural Ethiopia, seven out of 10 women had been attacked. Only in Japan was the figure less than 20 per cent.

- A 2002 WHO study puts the number of women physically abused by their partners or ex-partners at 30 per cent in the United Kingdom, and 22 per cent in the United States.

- A study conducted in São Paulo, Brazil, reported that 13 per cent of deaths of women of reproductive age were homicides, of which 60 per cent were committed by the victims' partners.

- In Guatemala, between 2001 and 2007, almost 4,000 women were murdered. Homicides of women have increased by 56 per cent during this period. Every two days, a young girl dies a violent death.

- According to a UNIFEM report on violence against women in Afghanistan, out of 1,327 incidents of violence against women collected between January 2003 and June 2005, 36 women had been killed – in 16 cases (44.4 per cent) by their intimate partners.

Krug et al. 2002, 'World Report on Violence and Health', Geneva: WHO. 90-91, reported in www.unifem.org/gender_issues; Referred to by SG Diniz, AF d'Oliveira, *International Journal of Gynecology and Obstetrics*, 63 Suppl. 1 (1998), reported in www.unifem.org; UNIFEM Afghanistan, Julie Lafreniere, 'Uncounted and Discounted: A Secondary Data Research Project on Violence against Women in Afghanistan', 2006.

Violence against women has economic as well as social consequences. The US Centers for Disease Control and Prevention (CDC) estimates that the costs of intimate partner violence in the United States alone exceed $5.8 billion per year: $4.1 billion are for direct medical and health care services, while productivity losses account for nearly $1.8 billion.[6] In a recent survey by the American Institute on Domestic Violence, 60 per cent of senior executives said that nearly eight million days of paid work are lost each year through women being unable to turn up for work due to domestic violence.[7]

Domestic violence and the law

Laws against domestic violence are on the increase – in 2003, 45 countries had specific laws on the

No help at hand in the UK

One night, Tasneen Ahmed's husband finally went too far. She was used to him hitting her, but this time he didn't stop. While their small children looked on, he punched her repeatedly, pulled her about by her hair and, when she fell to the floor, started kicking her in the stomach. In hospital, the doctors said they would have to wait for the bruising on her face to go down before they could treat her injuries – a broken nose, a shattered cheekbone.

Ahmed (not her real name) avoids eye contact; her smile is a rare, fleeting thing. Speaking through an interpreter, she says: 'I was a happy woman when I left Pakistan. I came with great hopes into this country.' She starts quietly crying. 'After it all started, I thought: "Is this what my life is going to be like from now on? Am I never going to be happy?"'

Her decision to leave her husband and bring charges against him has put her in danger. It is not uncommon for women in her position to be threatened with violence. Yet despite these risks, she is not in a safe house or women's refuge. No organization in her adopted town of Rochdale, Greater Manchester, will take her in.

Ahmed is one of a little-known group of people classed as NRPF – No Recourse to Public Funds. In Britain on a two-year probationary visa, these women – primarily, but not solely, from the Asian subcontinent – have no right to public aid, even if a marriage breaks down because of violent abuse. With no money, often speaking little English and with little knowledge of Britain's laws, they are confronted with a brutal choice: stay in an abusive relationship in fear of their lives, or leave and face destitution.

Alexandra Topping, *The Guardian*, 23 January 2008, www.guardian.co.uk/society

subject, while by 2006 this had increased to 89.[8] But legislation alone does not seem to be enough to stop the violence, although at least it gives some women recourse to the law – if they can find a safe place to hide, and have enough funds, support and courage. In the 1990s many countries enacted specific domestic violence legislation; some were limited to civil law, providing routes to protection orders for the first time; some extended the ways protection orders and police powers could be used; some linked civil and criminal processes; some created new criminal offenses or changed the status of assaults in the home; some were forms of 'integrated law' that refer both to legal

A devastating toll

Nicole Kidman and the UN Fund to eliminate Violence Against Women

In 1996, the United Nations General Assembly established the UN Trust Fund in Support of Actions to Eliminate Violence Against Women. The Trust Fund is managed by UNIFEM and is the only multilateral grant-making mechanism that supports local, national and regional efforts to combat violence. Since it began operations in 1997, the Trust Fund has awarded more than $19 million to 263 initiatives to address violence against women in 115 countries. For example, it has funded:

- The Lawyers Collective in India, which works to help the Indian legal system adjust the ways it handles domestic abuse cases. In 2005, they were part of a campaign which successfully pushed through the Protection of Women from Domestic Violence Act.
- In Bolivia and Ecuador, the fund has supported indigenous women to counter domestic violence through the leadership of indigenous women's human rights advocates. Local people conduct community dialogues on the issue of violence and examine existing national laws to determine which parts both respect local cultures and protect women's rights. Backed by state resources and communities, this information is then used to devise local service and protection mechanisms.

Says UNIFEM Goodwill Ambassador and actress Nicole Kidman: 'The more I've learned about the people and organizations this Trust Fund supports, the more I've wanted to get involved. We all know in our heads and our hearts that every woman is entitled to a life free of violence. Let's make that a reality.'

www.unifem.org/campaigns

---

powers and state responsibilities in terms of funding services and set up monitoring/prevention projects under a system of statutory funding from the state.

States have tended to adopt a passive attitude when confronted by cases of violations of women's rights, especially when they occur within the home. What occurs between a man and a woman, especially when she is his wife, is seen as a 'private' matter. Even when laws against domestic violence exist, most fail to protect victims or to punish perpetrators. Often police are also complicit, and the law becomes very hard to enforce.

Passing laws to criminalize violence against women is an important way to redefine the limits of acceptable

New law but no change in Cambodia

Cambodia adopted its first law against domestic violence in 2005. 'After five years of work, people have begun to understand that domestic violence is not a private issue,' says Hor Phally, Director of the Project Against Domestic Violence. But almost three years later, the law has yet to be implemented: 'Women's rights are written in the constitution because we share equal rights with men, but it is not implemented,' said Seng Theary, executive director of the Center for Social Development.

'I do not believe in this law, it only exists on paper, because the law is not implemented nor enforced,' said a 30-year-old woman. 'When my husband is drunk, he uses his rights as a husband to beat me, until my head bleeds,' she said. 'Because I have children, I endured this for them.'

Hor Phally said men and women need to communicate better, and they should not resort to violence to solve their problems. Ung Chanthol, director of the Cambodian Women's Crisis Center, said one of the driving forces behind the problem is the lack of appropriate law enforcement. 'If we could have a 70 to 80 per cent increase [in law enforcement], it would help a lot,' she said. 'Instead, the perpetrators are not arrested.'

'Women, War and Peace', UNIFEM 2002; www.voanews.com/Khmer

behavior. In recent years, women have increasingly been using the law to seek redress.

Men against violence against women

But the law is not the only factor. Men are the perpetrators of such crimes against women. Many societies condone violence against women if it is committed by her husband. Changing this means a fundamental review of the relationships between men and women and the unequal power relationships that exist between them. 'Educating boys and men to view women as valuable partners in life, in the development of a society and in the attainment of peace are just as important as taking legal steps to protect women's human rights,'[9] says the United Nations. This is just as true in the US as it is in Turkey, or Brazil, or Senegal.

The need to involve men in the gender equality movement in support of women's empowerment was first explicitly articulated in the Cairo Plan of Action on Population and Development. Since then, it has been recognized as a powerful strategy to enhance the participation of men in programs and projects for gender equality. As (most) males are the beneficiaries of gender inequalities, they hold the keys to eliminating gender-based inequalities. They have the economic, moral, political, religious and social responsibility to combat all forms of gender discrimination and inequalities. This is true even in the most extreme cases, for example, with so-called 'honor killings' where a male member of the family kills a female member for supposed sexual misconduct that has disgraced the 'honor' of the family. In Turkey, for example, one study reports that 'the Directorate of Religious Affairs has issued a ruling asking all imams across Turkey to discuss honor crimes, and proclaim that they are not congruent with Islamic principles.'[10]

Women's rights activist Leyla Parvizat notes: 'In order to prevent honor killings, it is crucial to redefine the concept of honor within the community. When talking to families, a cultural discourse proves to be very effective. We believe that male members are also victims of the concept of masculinity – they suffer throughout the decision-making process. We try to give men what I call cultural and psychological space where their masculinity is not challenged and they do not feel forced to kill in order to cleanse their honor. To do this, and in order to create space for long-term change, we take advantage of some of the positive aspects of Turkish culture to offer individual men an excuse to avoid violence. These include special occasions and gatherings where nonviolence negotiations are encouraged or where authority figures can act as intermediaries, in which we can make use of traditions of hospitality towards guests or respect for elderly people's recommendations as tools to prevent these crimes.'[11]

There are increasing numbers of men's groups around the world to combat violence against women. The White Ribbon campaign, for example, where

Men against sexual assault

From the University of Rochester, US:

- Don't have sex with a person against their will.
- Make sure that the sex you are having is consensual.
- Take responsibility for your own actions.
- Watch out for your buddies and your friends when you go out to make sure that none of you get into bad situations.
- Communicate – talk with your partner to make sure that you are both on the same page.
- Talk with your friends – discuss issues such as rape and sexual assault, try to clear up any misconceptions or misunderstandings you may have.
- Educate yourself and those around you about sexual assault.
- Support organizations which fight to decrease the occurrence of sexual assault and rape.
- Don't condone rape jokes, speak up when you hear one and say that it is offensive.
- Believe what people tell you if they have been raped or know someone who has.
- Don't assume that women want your protection; however, offer it to them and be there for them if they do want it.
- Organize or join a group of men at your school, workplace or just with your friends to work against rape and sexual assault.

http://sa.rochester.edu/masa/

men wear a white ribbon to show their opposition to violence against women, has taken off in at least 47 countries.[12]

Female genital cutting

Other practices can also be considered a form of violence against women. Female genital cutting (FGC) is the most obvious of these. Sometimes called female genital mutilation (FGM), it is an operation to remove part or all of a girl's external genital organs.

Between 100 and 140 million women and girls are estimated to have undergone FGC between the time they were babies and 16 years old. A further two million girls are considered to be at risk. Most live in Africa, although some are in Asia and the Middle East. They are also increasingly found in Europe, Australia,

---

Types of female genital cutting
Type one – the removal of the clitoris
Type two – the removal of the clitoris and surrounding labia
Type three – known as infibulation, where all external genitalia are removed and the opening is stitched so that only a small hole remains.

Canada and the US, mainly among immigrants from these countries.[13]

FGC is sometimes referred to as 'female circumcision', and involves 'partial or total removal of the external female genitalia or other injury to the female genital organs whether for cultural, religious or other non-therapeutic reasons'.[14] It is often performed without anesthetic and with unsterilized instruments.

Female genital cutting is claimed by some Muslims to be an Islamic practice, but in fact it pre-dates Islam and is also practised by followers of other religious beliefs. Its proponents argue that it is cleaner and healthier, and that it prevents women from being 'promiscuous' and therefore is necessary for a good marriage. In some places it is considered part of cultural heritage. Girls who do not have the operation may find themselves unable to marry and their whole family ostracized.

FGC can have severe health consequences. The operation is often performed with crude tools in non-sterile circumstances. Immediate complications include severe pain, shock, hemorrhage, urine retention, ulceration of the genital region and injury to adjacent tissue. Hemorrhage and infection can cause death. There is concern about possible HIV transmission. Other long-term consequences include cysts and abscesses, scar formation, urinary incontinence, painful sexual intercourse, sexual dysfunction and difficulties with childbirth.

Change is slow and difficult. In Eritrea, over half the population opposes the practice – with slightly more than half the men and slightly less than half the women registering disapproval.

When saying 'I do' means saying 'I don't'.

At their wedding in Durame, capital of Kembata district, in Ethiopia, Genet Girma wore a placard around her neck which declared: 'I am not circumcized, learn from me.' The bridegroom, Adissie Abossie, carried one which read: 'I am proud to marry an uncircumcized woman.' Just how brave Girma and Abossie were in deciding to celebrate their marriage by taking a public stand against the practice of female genital cutting (FGC) is hard to appreciate without some idea of how widespread the practice is. Ninety per cent of women in Ethiopia have had the operation. But attitudes to FGC in Ethiopia and elsewhere are slowly changing due to governmental and non-governmental interventions. The Kembata Women's Self-Help Centre (KMG), for instance, has been quietly working to eradicate FGC since 1997 by educating young girls and their families about its dangers.

Its school and community-based workshops and individual follow-ups have led some 4,000 women and girls to sign a pledge against FGC – and Girma was one of them. 'The reason I was able to avoid being circumcized is because of the training I took through KMG,' says Girma, who persuaded her parents to delay the procedure. Another incentive was her fiancé's strong opposition. 'He told me that if I am circumcized he wouldn't marry me,' she adds. Abossie knew from personal experience the suffering FGC causes. 'I was the first child and I could see how difficult [subsequent] deliveries were for my mother,' he explains. Women who have experienced the most extreme form of FGC must be cut open and re-sewn after every birth. 'After I understood that it resulted from circumcision, I decided not to marry a circumcized girl.'

Other couples have now taken the same decision. KMG founder Dr Bogalech Gebre is thrilled, saying 'every [anti-FGC] wedding is becoming a forum for education' – but notes that 'change must come from within'.

Gebre, who was cut at the age of six, has said: 'I understood the purpose [of] female genital excision was to excise my mind, excise my ability to live with all my senses intact.' One girl-child most definitely not at risk is Girma's and Abossie's two-month-old daughter. She is called Wimma, which means full or complete.

Abinet Aseffa, Panos features, www.panos.org.uk

There have been other success stories – according to the UN Secretary-General, 'by April 2006, 15 of the 28 African states where FGM is prevalent made it an offense under criminal law. Of the nine states in Asia and the Arabian Peninsula where female genital mutilation/cutting is prevalent among certain groups, two have enacted legal measures prohibiting it. In

A devastating toll

addition, 10 states in other parts of the world have enacted laws criminalizing the practice.'[15]

Violence in conflict situations

According to Amnesty International, 'Women are in double jeopardy... Few countries treat their women as well as their men... While women are under-represented in national and international decision-making structures, they are over-represented among the victims of human rights abuse.'[16] This young woman commander in war-torn Liberia adds: 'I would like to tell other people about the war and what we have been through. I want to tell them, even the whole world. We the women should tell the world what happened to us and what they did to us. I think that women even should have the highest positions. If they like me I will do it. But first I have to finish school. Now I'm still in ninth grade.'[17]

As a response to these sorts of situations, UN Resolution 1325 on Women, Peace and Security 'calls on all actors involved, when negotiating and implementing peace agreements, to adopt a gender perspective' and 'invites the Secretary-General to carry out a study on the impact of armed conflict on women and girls, the role of women in peace-building and the gender dimensions of peace processes and conflict resolution.'

Table 13 – Conflict-related deaths

The 20th century saw an unprecedented rise in the number of people dying in wars – increasing numbers of these are women and children as civilians bear an ever-larger burden of the death toll.

16th century	1.6	million
17th century	6.1	million
18th century	7.0	million
19th century	19.4	million
20th century	109.7	million

World report on violence and health, WHO 2002.

This is much needed. The 20th century was the most violent in history. Nearly 110 million people died as the result of conflict and war. Some 310,000 people were killed in wars in 2000 alone. Sixty per cent of these were civilians. For every person killed directly in a conflict, nine more are likely to die of starvation or disease.

And women are the new victims of this escalation. Where previously it was mainly soldiers who died, civilians are now deliberately targeted in large numbers – the percentage of civilians killed and wounded as a result of hostilities has risen from five per cent of casualties at the turn of the last century, to 65 per cent during the Second World War and 90 per cent in more recent conflicts. Eighty per cent of these victims are women and children.[18] At the end of 2006, there were 32.9 million refugees and internally displaced people in the world; 50 per cent of these were women and 50 per cent children under 18.[19]

Women experience the horrors of war in different ways from men. They too face death, mostly as non-combatants, but they also suffer sexual violence, forced rape and resultant pregnancy, abduction and sexual abuse and slavery. At the same time they are responsible for their families. Marion, aged 17, from Sierra Leone, tells her story:

'My family and I were hiding in a room during an attack when a rebel broke in. My mother was asked to give one of her children up or else the entire family would be killed. My mother gave me up. The rebels took me with them, and on our way to their camp I was raped by seven of them. I was bleeding heavily and unable to walk any further. They threatened to kill me if I did not go with them. I was held by them for one year. After I escaped, I asked myself: "Who will help me now?"'[20]

A devastating toll

The consequences of rape in Darfur

I am 16 years old. One day, in March 2004, I was collecting firewood for my family when three armed men on camels came and surrounded me. They held me down and tied my hands and raped me one after the other. When I arrived home, I told my family what happened. They threw me out of the home and I had to build my own hut away from them. I was engaged to a man and I was so much looking forward to getting married. After I got raped, he did not want to marry me and broke off the engagement because he said I was now disgraced and spoilt. It is the worst thing for me...

When I was eight months pregnant from the rape, the police came to my hut and forced me with their guns to go to the police station. They asked me questions so I told them I had been raped. They told me that as I was not married I would deliver the baby illegally. They beat me with a whip on the chest and back and put me in jail. There were other women in jail who had the same story. During the day, we had to walk to the well four times a day to get the policemen water, clean and cook for them. At night I was in one small cell with 23 other women. I had no other food than what I could find during my work during the day. And the only water was what I drank at the well. I stayed 10 days in the jail and now I have to pay the fine, 20,000 Sudanese dinars ($65) they asked from me. My child is now two months old.

Woman, 16, February 2005, West Darfur
8 March 2005, 'The Crushing Burden of Rape: Sexual Violence in West Darfur', Médecins sans Frontières, 8 March 2005,
www.doctorswithoutborders.org

Deliberate targets

The deliberate infection of women with HIV/AIDS has given a new twist to the spread of the pandemic. Women have increasingly been intended targets in other ways as well; the use of brutal mass rape against women and girls is an increasingly common tactic in modern warfare – often with the purpose of making them pregnant with the rapist's child as a form of ethnic domination (see box). Women's bodies have become part of the battlefield. In Darfur, in Sudan, for example, Amnesty International says: 'Abuses against women are an integral part of the conflict and are too often neglected.'[21] The UN says that around 40 per cent of the victims have been under 18 years of age.[22]

Like the young woman in the 'Darfur' box (p. 116), women who have been raped may face the added persecution of being rejected by their families and possibly of becoming pregnant by the rapists.

The shame and stigma that women face in such circumstances merely add to their suffering. Women may be coming home to very traditional families and communities, who believe, rightly or wrongly, that their wives, sisters and daughters have been sexually abused, have brought 'dishonor' on the family and are therefore no longer marriageable. They may be returning to homes where they fled violence in the first place. In addition, recent evidence has shown that they are also assaulted by the international peacekeepers who are supposed to protect them. In 2005, seven UN agencies received 373 new sexual exploitation and abuse allegations, of which 340 involved UN peacekeeping personnel.[23]

Legal successes

There have been a number of historic legal successes in the last few years for women who have suffered during war.

First, the designation of rape and enslavement as crimes against humanity. On 22 February 2001 the International Criminal Tribunal for the former Yugoslavia (ICTY) convicted Dragoljub Kunarac, Radomir Kovac, and Zoran Vukovic for rape, torture, and enslavement. It was an historic moment for women's rights – the first time in history that an international tribunal had convicted on the basis of crimes of sexual violence against women.

Regan Ralph, Director of the Women's Rights Division of Human Rights Watch, said: 'Finally, the international community is taking these sexual crimes – rapes, gang rapes, and sexual enslavement of women – seriously. This interpretation will serve as the basis to prosecute others who enslave women around the world.'[24]

A devastating toll

Second, the establishment of the International Criminal Court (ICC) in July 2002, though marred by American refusal to take part, was another victory for women's rights activists. Rape, sexual slavery, enforced prostitution, forced pregnancy, enforced sterilization, sexual violence, and persecution on account of gender were defined in the ICC statutes as war crimes and crimes against humanity. The ICC Rules offer important protections for victims and witnesses, particularly those who suffered sexual or gender violence. Six of the top seven judges on the new International Criminal Court are women. 'It's completely historic,' said Vahida Nainar, of the Women's Caucus for Gender Justice. 'It's the first time for international courts. In 85 years the International Court of Justice has had just one woman judge.' [25]

Third, the establishment of a Women's International War Crimes Tribunal 2000, which sat in Tokyo, Japan. Run by non-governmental organizations, this was established to consider the criminal liability of leading high-ranking Japanese military and political officials and the separate responsibility of the State of Japan for rape and sexual slavery as crimes against humanity arising out of Japanese military activity in the Asia-Pacific region in the 1930s and 1940s. It had been a long time in the making, and many of the elderly women making submissions had never talked about their suffering before.

Fourth, the Truth and Reconciliation Commissions. In the last 15 years there have been 24 such commissions. Truth commissions are 'bodies established to research and report on human rights abuses over a certain period of time in a particular country or in relation to a particular conflict.' The most famous is probably the one in South Africa to investigate abuses under apartheid, where many women testified.[26] In Sierra Leone, where a commission was established in 2000 to investigate such actions during the war, the abuse of women's human rights was specifically singled out and young people brought out their own version of the report.

And finally, as a result of the reports of abuse in 2002, then UN Secretary-General Kofi Annan issued a bulletin entitled 'Special Measures for Protection from Sexual Exploitation and Sexual Abuse for all UN personnel' which laid out disciplinary measures that would be taken if peacekeepers abused women in the communities they had come to protect.

Women and peace-building

In the words of Noeleen Heyzer, former executive director of the UN's women's agency, UNIFEM, 'The involvement of women in peace-building and reconstruction is a key part of the process of inclusion and democracy that can contribute to a lasting peace.'[27]

Women have particular needs in times of war. Their voices are often not heard when it comes to peace-building, as few are in positions to make decisions. Over the last decades there has been an expansion of women's peace groups. Some have a long history – the International Congress of Women goes back to World War One, when women from 12 countries braved the war to meet and discuss how to end the

---

Table 14 – No protection, no safety

The increasing reports of sexual abuse by UN troops are a major cause for concern.

UN peacekeepers sexual abuse scandals

2003 – Nepalese troops accused of sexual abuse while serving in DR Congo. Six are later jailed

2004 – Two UN peacekeepers repatriated after being accused of abuse in Burundi

2005 – UN troops accused of rape and sexual abuse in Sudan

2006 – UN personnel accused of rape and exploitation on missions is Haiti and Liberia

2007 – UN launches probe into sexual abuse claims in Côte d'Ivoire

http://news.bbc.co.uk/1/hi/world/africa/6909664.stm

Seeds of Peace

At age 13, Bushra Jawabri began representing schools in Arroub refugee camp on the occupied West Bank, in meetings with Israelis, presenting the Palestinian perspective on various issues of the conflict. Julia Resnitsky left Russia at age seven when her family moved as refugees to Jerusalem. In high school, she organized nonviolent conflict resolution workshops for junior high students.

Bushra and Julia have been involved in Seeds of Peace, an international organization that helps teenagers from conflict regions learn peace-making skills. In November 2001 Bushra was part of the official Palestinian delegation at the New York City International Youth Conference on uprooting the causes of hatred and terror, which was organized in response to the attacks of 11 September. Julia's leadership in peace issues is challenged by her community, friends and family, who do not support her beliefs, yet she continues to volunteer with disadvantaged Palestinian and Israeli youth and mentor friends to work towards peaceful co-existence regardless of the obstacles they face.

Both girls were among those awarded the Voices of Courage award by the Women's Commission for Refugee Women and Children in 2002. Bushra said on receiving the award: 'Keeping faith and staying optimistic towards peace have not been easy. But truly what kept the hope of peace alive in my heart is exchanging emails and phone calls with my Israeli friends, friends who I met through the Seeds of Peace camp. They kept me optimistic towards peace, towards a better future, people like Julia. It was very important for me to hear Julia condemning inhumane actions done by anyone, no matter what his or her nationality is. And I always ask myself, why do I have to witness innocent civilian Palestinians getting killed every day? Why do I have to witness innocent Israeli civilians getting killed every day? Why did I have to witness three thousand Americans killed on September 11? The answer is this, I believe. It is my task, my mission, a task that we all have to follow, which is to work for a better future, if not for ourselves, for our children.'

www.unfpa.org/swp/2005 and www.womenscommission.org/voices

carnage. This group eventually became the Women's International League for Peace and Freedom, which now has branches throughout the world. Some go back decades – in 1988, women in Israel gathered to stand silently on the street to protest against their country's occupation of the West Bank and Gaza and to show their solidarity with Palestinian women. They stood at the same time each week, each day, silent and dressed all in black. Sometimes they were insulted and abused; sometimes people came to shake their hands. They were followed by women in many countries of the world and today Women in Black groups exist not only in Israel but in Azerbaijan, Canada, Denmark, England, France, India, Indonesia, Italy, Scotland, Spain, Switzerland and Turkey.

Some are more recent – in 2003, women were at the forefront of anti-war marches, when over 30 million people around the world showed their objection to the US and UK's war against Iraq.

Violence against women is essentially about power; the power that men have over women. The next chapter looks at the changing nature of relationships between the sexes and the issue of sexuality.

1 www.unifem.org/gender_issues 2 General Assembly, 'In-Depth Study on All Forms of Violence against Women: Report of the Secretary General, 2006', A/61/122/Add.1, 6 July 2006, reported in www.unifem.org/gender_issues 3 ibid. 4 Parliamentary Assembly of the Council of Europe 2002, Recommendation 1582 (2002) on Domestic Violence against Women, reported in www.unifem.org/gender_issues 5 Referred to by UNAIDS, UNFPA, UNIFEM; *Women and HIV/AIDS: Confronting the Crisis*. Geneva, New York. 2004. 6 Centers for Disease Control and Prevention, 2003, 'Costs of Intimate Partner Violence against Women in the United States', Atlanta, reported in www.unifem.org/gender_issues 7 American Institute on Domestic Violence. 2001, Domestic Violence in the Workplace Statistics. 8 www.unifem.org/gender_issues 9 The United Nations Department of Public Information DPI/1772/HR-February 1996. 10 Nuket Kardam and Yannis Toussulis 'Religion and conflict: lessons from the frontlines of Social Transformation in Women's Human Rights', in Policy Perspectives, Islam and Tolerance in Wider Europe, IPF 2006. 11 Parvizat, Leyla, 'In the Name of Honor', Human Rights Dialgoue, Fall 2003, quoted in Nuket Kardam and Yannis Toussulis 'Religion and conflict: lessons from the frontlines of Social Transformation in Women's Human Rights', in Policy Perspectives, Islam and Tolerance in Wider Europe, IPF 2006. 12 www.whiteribbon.com 13 www.who.int/inf-fs/en/fact241.html 14 WHO definition. 15 General Assembly, 'In-Depth Study on All Forms of Violence against Women: Report of the Secretary-General', 2006; A/61/122/Add.1. 6 July 2006. 40. 16 March 1995 (AI Index: ACT 77/01/95). 17 Ibid. 18 www.savethechildren.org 19 www.unhcr.org/statistics/STATISTICS 20 Conference on Sexual and Gender-based violence, Geneva, 27-29 March 2001, UNHCR. 21 Amnesty International report AI Index: AFR 54/076/2004 Sudan, Darfur A Weapon of War: Sexual Violence and its consequences. 22 UN Security Council Report on Children and Armed Conflict, 26 October 2006 http://daccessdds.un.org/doc/UNDOC/GEN 23 'Women, War, Peace: The Independent Experts' Assessment on the Impact of Armed Conflict on Women and Women's Role in Peace-Building' (Progress of the World's Women 2002, Vol. 1) by Elisabeth

A devastating toll

Rehn, Ellen Johnson-Sirleaf. www.unifem.org/attachments/products **24** www.hrw.org/press/2001/02/serbia0222.htm **25** Chris Stephen, *The Observer*, 9 February 2003. **26** www.doj.gov.za/trc/hrvtrans/index.htm **27** www.unfpa.org/swp/2005/english/ch8/index.htm

9 Marriage, sexuality and old age

'I never ever understand why boys and girls are not equal to each other. In rural areas elders think that girls are born to give birth and to marry and for cleaning the house. Girls who live in rural areas... are not sent to schools. Their parents are not aware of the changing world yet'. GIRL, AGED 15, TURKEY.[1]

Relationships are changing. Households are smaller, more are headed by women, and more people live on their own. Eighty-five per cent of lone-parent households are headed by women. But the majority of women still live under the control of their husbands. Far too many marry at a very young age. And for those who do not conform, life can be hard.

FAMILIES ARE CHANGING. And so are relationships between men and women.[2] Households are getting smaller; there are larger numbers of lone parents and more people than ever are living on their own. In the North, fewer people are getting married – out-of-marriage births have increased more than 50 per cent in the last 20 years.

While most women still spend the majority of their lives married, divorce is also on the increase – in Belarus, Russia, Sweden, Latvia and Ukraine there are more divorces than there are marriages. In a number of countries in the last few years, same-sex marriage has become legally possible.

Other things have changed very little. Despite legislation in many countries against early marriage, more than a fifth of women in the poorest regions of the world already have a child by the time they are 18. In Western and Middle Africa and South Central and Southeast Asia, 58 per cent of women are married before they are 18.[3]

Marriage, sexuality and old age

Table 15 – Marrying young

In Western and Central Africa and South Central and Southeast Asia, 58 per cent of women are married before they are 18. When a woman is married young, she loses out on schooling and her choices may be limited by having many children.

Married girls aged 15-19

UN Population Division, Department of Economic and Social Affairs, World Marriage Patterns 2000.

	Percentage
Sub-Saharan Africa	
Dem Rep of Congo	74
Niger	70
Congo	56
Uganda	50
Mali	50
Asia	
Afghanistan	54
Bangladesh	51
Nepal	42
Middle East	
Iraq	28
Syria	25
Yemen	24
Latin America and Caribbean	
Honduras	30
Cuba	29
Guatemala	24

In many countries, married women still 'belong' to their husbands and in some they need their husband's permission to buy or sell property, have an abortion, work, or even for traveling and opening a bank account. Most early marriages mean that the young bride has to leave school. In Swaziland, for example, married women are still legal minors, though under civil law they can sign a prenuptial agreement which gives them adult status. In Yemen, the law says that women must obey their husbands, live with him where he wants to live and not leave their home without his permission. In Kyrgyzstan the law prohibits divorce during pregnancy and while a child is less than a year old. In the north of Nigeria women can be flogged

Early marriage in selected countries

Rajasthan, India The custom survives of giving very small children away in marriage. On the auspicious day of *Akha Teej*, the mass solemnization of marriages between young boys and girls is performed. From the parents' point of view, this is the tried and tested way of organizing the passing on of property and wealth within the family.

Niger A study by UNICEF in six West African countries showed that 44 per cent of 20-24 year old women were married under the age of 15. The need to follow tradition, reinforce ties among or between communities, and protect girls from out-of-wedlock pregnancy were the main reasons given. In the communities studied, all decisions on timing of marriage and choice of spouse were made by the fathers.

Bangladesh Many Bangladeshi girls are married soon after puberty, partly to free their parents from an economic burden and partly to protect the girls' sexual purity. Where a girl's family is very poor or she has lost her parents, she may be married as a third or fourth wife to a much older man, to fulfill the role of sexual and domestic servant.

Albania Families in rural areas, reduced to abject poverty by the post-Communist transition, encourage their daughters to marry early in order to catch potential husbands before they migrate to the cities in search of work, and to avoid the threat of kidnapping on the way to school.

Niger A study conducted in a rural area of Niger in 2003 found that 68 per cent of girls were married before their first menstruation, and 52 per cent had a child before they reached the age of 16. Of those who had been married before the age of 16, only 16 per cent had received some education. Those who had married later had a much higher rate of schooling, with 42 per cent having received some education.

'Early marriage: child spouses', *Innocenti Digest* No 7 March 2001, UNICEF.

or stoned to death for adultery. And men all over the world are still beating their wives – and getting away with it (see chapter on violence).

In other parts of the world, the nature of marriage is beginning to change and legislation that gives women more rights within marriage is being pushed through. In Sri Lanka, where girls have traditionally been married young, the average age at marriage has now risen to 25 years. Much of this is due to changes in the law, which now requires that all marriages are registered and that the consent of both marriage partners is recorded. Improvements in health care and education for girls have also helped to push the age of marriage up.[4]

Sharing the burden at home

'It is not only a matter of women entering the social world more boldly... It is also a matter of men sharing life in the family's intimate world more fully,' said Alva Myrdal, back in 1944 in Sweden. While more women than ever before are working, men have still been largely reluctant to enter the domestic sphere and share in tasks like housework and childcare.

In the US in 1965, men spent 12 hours a week on cooking, cleaning and other housework and compared with 16 hours today. That is an extra hour per decade. In Sweden, men do 24 hours and women 33. And in Japan, men do six hours and women 29. Elsewhere, research shows that between two and 12 per cent of men now do an equal share of housework. In South Asia, women spent three to five hours more than men each week on subsistence activities such as carrying water and wood, and between 20 and 30 hours more on housework.[5]

In the 1990s Australia became the first country to attempt to quantify this unpaid work and the calculations suggest that its value was equivalent to 58 per cent of Gross Domestic Product.[6]

Psychologists Claire Rabin and Pepper Schwartz found that when wives and husbands make what they both feel is a successful effort to divide chores fairly, both spouses benefit. Inequities in housework and childcare have profound consequences for the marital satisfaction of women, which in turn affects the quality of the marriage for the man as well.

But any equality often goes out the window once a couple have children. Says British political commentator Polly Toynbee: 'Young women outshining boys at school have a habit of thinking all the great feminist causes are won: but once they become mothers and are shocked to find it isn't so, they are too exhausted to do anything about it.'[7] Lack of childcare is still a big problem through most of the Western world. Although grandmothers often help with childcare, it is mainly the responsibility of the parents, and usually the mother. And yet school days and work days rarely coincide, and state nursery provision is very patchy.

This may well become a problem for men as well. At present, men are still seen as the main breadwinners, and many are working longer rather than shorter days, leading to conflict with family needs. It is not just high-profile women who leave their jobs to 'be with their families' these days, but high-profile men as well. There has been a revolution for women in the workplace; now there needs to be a revolution which embraces both men and women at home.

Men and women

It seems that while women have changed a lot, men's behavior patterns towards women have changed very little. Susan Faludi, author of *Backlash: the war against women*, believes that improvements in women's lives are dependent not just on women themselves, but on men changing the way they behave: 'I would hope that men could grapple with the true nature of their burden and see that it's shared by women, and that men and women could find common ground to fight the forces that demean them both.'[8] Recognizing that entrenched attitudes begin at a young age, there are many projects working with young men as well as young women to help them look at their attitudes towards relationships.

In Rio de Janeiro in Brazil, for example, 'male involvement in reproductive health and childcare is limited; men generally feel that they are entitled to sex from women; tolerance of violence against women is fairly widespread.'

The projects identified what factors were seen as

'gender equitable' and then held group discussions about life histories to help the young men see the 'costs' of traditional masculinities. Courses in Afro-Brazilian dance, computing and health promotion aim to encourage vocational and cultural competencies. Community awareness-raising about domestic violence targeted men and women whilst group formation was initiated and encouraged.

In South Africa and Nicaragua, similar projects with young men encourage them to examine and change traditional male behaviors. The HIV/AIDS epidemic has brought a new urgency to work with young men to encourage them to practice safe sexual behaviors and part of this is having more equitable relationships with women. Because young people's peer groups are a major influence, there are a wide range of peer-education projects, media-awareness campaigns and other initiatives like youth and sports clubs. A young man in Portugal, after one such program, noted: 'There are certain rights that are funda-mental. Sexual and reproductive rights are one of those. The attitude we should adopt concerning sexual and reproductive rights is to be conscious and respon-sible so we can make those rights a reality. That's our obligation. When I say OUR, I mean both men and women.'[9]

Sex education is fundamental here. In the Nether-lands, where sex education starts early and focuses on relationships as much as sex itself, the country has one of the lowest rates of teenage pregnancy in Europe and 56 per cent of young men cited 'love and commitment' as a reason for first sexual intercourse. Research-ers noted that 'since initial sex was more likely to occur within an emotional relationship, it was highly likely that there was... respect for the other's wishes.' Seventy-eight per cent of young men thought about pregnancy and 40 per cent were likely to talk about it with their partners. This compares with 57 per cent and 15 per cent in the UK, which has the highest rate of teenage pregnancy in Europe.[10]

Gay rights are women's rights

While same-sex marriage is gradually being permitted in a number of Western countries, elsewhere attitudes to gays and lesbians continue to lead to repression and persecution. In February 2007, for example, the Nigerian House of Representatives proposed a bill that would criminalize all expressions and forms of homosexuality. It included penalties of five years' imprisonment for any individual possessing or purchasing lesbian, gay, bisexual, or transgender (LGBT) literature or films, subscribing or donating to a LGBT organization, attending LGBT events, or expressing any form of same-sex desire. Advocates of the bill suggested that homosexuality is contradictory to conservative Nigerian cultural and religious beliefs.[11]

'Lesbian, gay, bisexual, and transgender people have been vilified by presidents and political leaders, which has led to a culture of intolerance,' said Paula Ettelbrick, executive director of International Gay and Lesbian Human Rights Commission. 'These attacks are just the first step in creating a climate in which all rights are at risk.'[12]

It is not easy being a lesbian. Around two per cent of the world's women live exclusively as homosexuals. Many more are forced to keep their sexuality secret. In 85 countries being homosexual is illegal and in seven

---

The bad news...
- In 85 countries homosexuality is illegal. In some countries, homosexuality is punishable under law by the death sentence. This includes Iran, Saudi Arabia, Mauritania, Sudan and Yemen and parts of Nigeria, Somalia, Pakistan, Iraq and Chechyna where sharia law is applied.

And the good...
- Homosexuality is legal in 111 countries.
- A number of these allow gay marriage.

Muslim countries it can mean life imprisonment or even execution. Members of the Bush Administration in the US also hold anti-gay views. Right-wing Senator Rick Santorum said: 'If the Supreme Court says that you have the right to consensual (gay) sex within your home, then you have the right to bigamy, you have the right to polygamy, you have the right to incest, you have the right to adultery. You have the right to anything.' The American Christian Right has an active lobby against what it sees as 'immoral and irrational' practices. Gary De Mar, from American Vision, an organization 'dedicated to Restoring America's Biblical Foundations', asks: 'Does it ever register with homosexuals that maybe God is telling them something when they get life-threatening diseases because of their sexual practices and can have no children no matter how hard they try? Like Dr Frankenstein, homosexuals take God's design of marriage and manufacture an artificial monster from its parts.'[13]

Often, repressive attitudes towards homosexuality are matched by repressive laws about women's rights in general, as in Saudi Arabia, where women are severely restricted and homosexuality can be punished by death. As we saw earlier, in some cultures, young women who are believed to have infringed family and social codes have been murdered by the male members of their family. This is sometimes known as 'honor killing'. A girl may have a boyfriend that her family does not approve of, she may refuse to have an arranged marriage, she may be a lesbian, or she may have been raped. Such killings have been reported in Afghanistan, Bangladesh, Britain, Brazil, Ecuador, Egypt, India, Israel, Italy, Jordan, Pakistan, Morocco, Sweden, Turkey and Uganda and Northern countries into which people from these countries have immigrated.

Ageing

'The meaning or lack of meaning that old age takes on in any given society puts the whole society to the test.' There are 650 million people over 60 in the world today. By 2050, this is forecast to reach two billion, 80 per cent of whom will live in the countries of the South. And a large proportion will be women, because, in general, women still live longer than men.

Among the oldest age groups, women outnumber men two to one. But life expectancy varies hugely from country to country. A female baby born in Iceland in 2005 can expect to live to 83, while one born in Sierra Leone can only expect to live to 43. In some countries, particularly those affected by HIV, life expectancy is actually going down.[14]

This 'gray revolution' will have an enormous effect on women and on families and relationships. The largest increases in older populations have been occurring in Asia and Africa. By 2025, the proportion of women aged 60 or older will almost double in East and South-East Asia, Latin America and the Caribbean, and North Africa. Women are more likely to be widowed. In some countries, traditional widowhood practices can result in abuse and even violence. Widows have often spent long years caring for their husbands, and probably before then for their parents, and afterwards for their grandchildren. Grandmothers are often the main source of childcare in a world where the majority of women work. This is particularly true when one or both parents have to migrate in search of work, and in countries where large numbers of parents die of AIDS. And yet women in older age are often neglected both by analysts and policy makers. Given the changing demography across the world, this is likely to become an increasingly important issue.

Marriage, sexuality and old age

Table 16 – Long live women!

In the rich world, women are living longer, and longer than men. The picture is different in some Majority World countries where life expectancy for both men and women has fallen, partly as a result of HIV/AIDS, and wars.

Female life expectancy at birth, 2005 (countries ranked by Human Development Index ranking)

Human Development Report 2007, UNDP http://hdrstats.undp.org/indicators/270.html

Top 10

1	Iceland	83.1
2	Norway	82.2
3	Australia	83.3
4	Canada	82.6
5	Ireland	80.9
6	Sweden	82.7
7	Switzerland	83.7
8	Japan	85.7
9	Netherlands	81.4
10	France	83.7

Bottom 10

168	Congo (Democratic Republic of the)	47.1
169	Ethiopia	53.1
170	Chad	51.8
171	Central African Republic	45.0
172	Mozambique	43.6
173	Mali	55.3
174	Niger	54.9
175	Guinea-Bissau	47.5
176	Burkina Faso	52.9
177	Sierra Leone	43.4

1 'Adolescent girls: the time for action is now!' What Young People Are Saying. Bi-monthly Newsletter of Voices of Youth, No 20, UNICEF, February 2006. Available at: www.unicef.org/voy/media/news.2006-02.doc .UNICEF, February 2006. **2** All the following information from *The Atlas of Women*, Joni Seager, Earthscan 2005. **3** Ibid. **4** *Children, Law and Justice. A South Asian Perspective*, Savitri Goonesekere, UNICEF-ICDC, Sage Publications, New Delhi, 1998, p 117 & 324 quoted in 'Early Marriage, child spouses' Innocenti Digest No 7 March 2001 http://www.unicef-irc.org/publications/pdf/digest7e.pdf **5** *The Atlas of Women in the World*, Joni Seager, Earthscan 2005. **6** Australian Bureau of Statistics 1994. **7** 'The mother of all issues' in *The Guardian*, 6 June 2003. **8** *Mother Jones* interview with Susan Faludi, by Susan Halpern, 1999. **9** www.ippf.org/resource/index.htm **10** cited in *Beyond victims and villains: addressing sexual violence in the education sector*, Judy Mirsky, Panos 2003. **11** http://feminist.org/news/newsbyte/uswirestory.asp?id=10176 **12** http://hrw.org/press/2003/05/safrica051403.htm **13** www.americanvision.org/ **14** www.who.int/features/factfiles/ageing/en/index.html

10 Conclusion: our president is a woman

'This is not the time to retreat from the fight for women's equality. It's the time, with sensitivity but also firmness, to step it up wherever we find prejudice. The prize is not just a better world for women. It is a better world for all.' CHERIE BOOTH, UK BARRISTER.[1]

Much of this book has shown how so many women still live in situations of great hardship and oppression. But the strides forward that they have made were achieved as a result of thousands of women's groups and organizations around the world refusing to give up the struggle for a better world for all. And young women are now in the forefront of change.

IT DOES NOT always feel like it, especially if you are poor, female and live in a shanty town in the South, but there have been many successes for women during the last few years; successes that have benefited both sexes. More girls than ever are at school; homosexuality is legal in 111 countries; women in the Anglican Church are now allowed to become vicars (priests) and even bishops; a number of countries have banned female circumcision; many have passed laws banning discrimination in the workplace; women have been appointed all over the world (though still in small numbers) as parliamentarians, judges and top executives. There has been a sea change in many countries in the way women are viewed; the younger generation of Western women, though they may not always acknowledge it, have benefited from the battles fought by their mothers and by all the millions of women around the world who have struggled to put their rights, and those of their sisters, firmly on the agenda at local, national and international levels.

Conclusion

Changing times

From the small to the sweeping, there have been changes since 2000 in many countries that have improved women's lives.[2]

Malaysia 2000 Women lawyers allowed to wear trousers in court.

Brazil 2001 Brazil passes changes to the Civil Code granting equal rights to women in marriage and divorce, in household decision-making authority, and a wide range of family matters.

Netherlands 2001 Gay and lesbian marriages granted full recognition on equal terms with heterosexual marriages.

Turkey 2001 The Turkish parliament revises the Civil Code to recognize women's equality. Women no longer need their husband's permission to work outside the home. Married women enjoy property rights and are allowed to keep their maiden name after marriage.

UK 2001 The 'morning-after' contraceptive pill becomes available without prescription for women over 16.

Iran 2002 Parliament approves a bill granting women the right to seek a divorce in court.

Lithuania 2002 The government repeals a requirement that women undergo a gynecological examination to qualify for a driver's license.

Norway 2002 Government orders companies to ensure that at least 40 per cent of the board members are women.

Vietnam 2002 Government bans polygamy and dowries in marriage.

Kuwait 2005 Women are allowed to vote in national elections for the first time.

Pakistan 2006 Women's Protection bill promises some progress for women on the legal front. Judges have been given the authority to try rape cases under criminal as opposed to Islamic sharia law. Women who have been raped no longer have to produce four witnesses.

Zimbabwe 2007 Domestic Violence Protection Act introduced to protect victims of domestic violence and provide long-term measures of prevention of domestic violence.

Liberia 2007 Introduces a law which imposes harsher penalties on perpetrators of rape and other sexual crimes against girls. The government also introduces legislation on inheritance which makes it a felony for anyone to force girls under 16 into marriage. Free and compulsory education at primary level has also becomes law.

Serbia 2007 Parliament passes a new law against domestic violence, as well as establishing inheritance rights for women.

In the beginning, women marched alone and organized as women's groups. But increasingly, they have been joined by men who see that change in favor of women will be for the benefit of both sexes. Men like those from the White Ribbon campaign against violence against women (see chapter 8), or the increasing numbers who take time off from work to look after their children, or those like Adisse Abossie, who take a stand against practices like female genital cutting (see chapter 8).

It is easy to forget just how recently so many women's rights have been won; and how many women still face violations of their rights on a daily basis.

Charting the changes for the better, but remembering how hard-won they have been, is a crucial part of holding back the tide that threatens, little by little, to sweep many of these achievements away. It is easy to forget, as well, just how far we have come. Sojourner Truth, ex-slave and activist, gave a speech in 1851 at the Women's Right's Convention in Ohio which boldly states that she is as good as any man, even in an age of slavery:

'That man over there says that women need to be helped into carriages and lifted over ditches and to have the best place everywhere. Nobody ever helps me into carriages, or over mud puddles or gives me any best place! And ain't I a woman? Look at me! Look at my arm! I have ploughed and planted and gathered into barns, and no man could head me! And ain't I a woman? I could work as much and eat as much as a man – when I could get it – and bear the lash as well!

16 Days of Activism Against Gender Violence

The 16 Days of Activism Against Gender Violence campaign is an international campaign started by the Center for Women's Global Leadership in the US in 1991. It runs from November 25, International Day Against Violence Against Women to December 10, International Human Rights Day, in order to symbolically link violence against women and human rights and to emphasize that such violence is a violation of human rights. Since 1991, approximately 1,700 organizations in 130 countries have participated. The Campaign has been used as an organizing strategy by individuals and groups around the world to call for the elimination of all forms of violence against women.

www.cwgl.rutgers.edu

Conclusion

And ain't I a woman? I have borne 13 children and seen most all sold off to slavery, and when I cried out with my mother's grief, none but Jesus heard me! And ain't I a woman?'

Today, it is young women who are in the forefront of change. While some still equate raunchiness with liberation, others are out there on the streets claiming their right not to be exploited; for example, a group of high school girls in Allegeny County, Pennsylvania, who organized a 'girlcott' of the Abercrombie and Fitch store when it produced a girl's shirt with the slogan across the breasts: 'WHO NEEDS BRAINS WHEN YOU HAVE THESE?' Media attention led to the company withdrawing the shirt.[3]

Or Akello Betty Openy and Ochora Emmanuel, adolescents displaced by the civil war in northern Uganda, who co-founded Gulu Youth for Action, a group that works to involve young people, especially girls, in issues of concern to them, such as adolescent health and education advocacy. Betty is one of eight young people chosen by Olara Otunnu, Special Representative of the UN Secretary-General on Children in Armed Conflict, to work with him to develop a youth advisory council with representatives from both war-ravaged and peaceful countries. 'Girls in my country keep to themselves and are quiet. A girl like myself can stand up for herself and advocate for others. I now have the confidence to talk to policy makers about girls' rights. I want to continue to help other girls gain the same confidence,' she says.[4]

Or Nasly Cubillos, who is 17 and comes from Aguablanca, a poor district in Calli, Colombia. One day in 2004 she found herself representing the youth of Latin America at a packed auditorium in Barcelona. It was the beginning of the Global Movement for Children, a worldwide movement of organizations and people.[5]

It is young women like these who will build that

better future. They have a hard task on their hands. I would like to end with a story told to Ellen Johnson-Sirleaf, the first-ever African woman president. A little girl playing with boys in a school is reprimanded for being rowdy. The principal says: 'You are a little girl; you should be quiet and not running around making such a noise.' The little girl ponders for a few seconds and says quietly: 'Teacher, be careful how you talk to me. Don't forget our President is a woman.'[6]

Change may be slow, it may be two steps forward and one step back, but it is on its way.

1 *The Observer*, 28 January 2007. **2** *Atlas of Women*, Joni Seager, Earthscan 2005. **3** *Full Frontal Feminism: A Young Woman's Guide to why Feminism Matters*, Jessica Valenti, Seal Press, 2007. **4** '15 years of advocacy and action', The Women's Commission for Refugee Women and Children, 2004, www.womenscommission.org/pdf/15_fix.pdf **5** 'Grassroots efforts to prevent and resolve violence', World Vision, 2005, www.justice-and-peace.org/PolicyAdvocacy **6** State of the World's Girls 2008, Plan.

Contacts and resources

INTERNATIONAL

Association for Women's Rights in Development (AWID)
Email: contact@awid.org
Website: www.awid.org

DAWN (Development Alternatives with Women for a New Era)
Email: info@dawnnet.org
Website: www.dawnnet.org

Human Rights Watch
Email: hrwnyc@hrw.org
Website: www.hrw.org/women

Amnesty International
Website: www.amnesty.org

ISIS (information and communication between women)
Website: www.isiswomen.org

UNIFEM – United Nations Development Fund for Women
Website: www.unifem.org

Women in Black
Website: www.womeninblack.net

Women's International League for Peace and Freedom (WILPF)
Email: wilpf@iprolink.ch
Website: www.wilpf.int.ch

Women Living Under Muslim Laws
Email: wluml@wluml.org
Website: www.wluml.org

Siyanda (online database of useful materials plus space for sharing ideas, experiences and resources.)
Website: www.siyanda.org

UK

Women Against Fundamentalisms
Email: nadje@gn.apc.org
Website: www.waf@gn.apc.org

Women's Environmental Network
Email:info@wen.org.uk
Website: www.wen.org.uk

WOMANKIND Worldwide

Email: info@womankind.org.uk
Website: www.womankind.org.uk

UNITED STATES

Bridge
Website: www.feministing.com

National Organization of Women
Email: now@now.org
Website: www.now.org

Third Wave Foundation
Email: info@thirdwavefoundation.org
Website: www.thirdwavefoundation.org

Women's Environment and Development Organization (WEDO)
Email: wedo@wedo.org
Website: www.wedo.org

Books and magazines

The Atlas of Women, Joni Seager, Earthscan 2005.
Backlash: the Undeclared War on Women, Susan Faludi, Chatto and Windus 1991.
Female Chauvinist Pigs: Women and the rise of Raunch Culture, Ariel Levy, Pocket Books 2006.
Feminism: a very short introduction, Margaret Walters, Oxford University Press 2005.
Focus on Gender series, edited by Caroline Sweetman, Oxfam. www.oxfam.org.uk
Full Frontal Feminism: a young woman's guide to why feminism matters, Jessica Valenti, Seal Press, 2007

Making Space for Indigenous Feminism, Joyce Green, Zed Books 2007.
The New Feminism, Natasha Walter, Virago 1999.
The No-Nonsense Guide to Sexual Diversity, Vanessa Baird, New Internationalist/BTL.
The Progress of Women 2002, UNIFEM.
The State of the World's Girls, Plan 2007 www.becauseiamagirl.org
The State of the World's Mothers, Save the Children.
Trouble and Strife, the radical feminist magazine http://troubleandstrife.org

Index

Index

Index